Menorca

Front cover: Cala Macarelleta

Right: The *taula* at Torralba d'en Salort

TOP 10 ATTRACTIONS

Binibeca Vell · A 'fishermen's village' designed for tourists *(page 79)*

Església de Santa Maria · Famed for its grand organ and one of the sights in the capital, Maó *(page 30)*

Cala Santa Galdana · A lovely cove, popular with families and watersports enthusiasts *(page 72)*

Plaça d'es Born · This square in Ciutadella is surrounded by some splendid mansions (page 59)

Ciutadella · The golden walls of the town rise above the harbour *(page 57)*

Parc Natural de S'Albufera · A haven for birdwatching and exploring the coastal environment *(page 41)*

Fornells · A pretty harbour and some tempting fish restaurants *(page 45)*

Naveta d'es Tudons · Believed to be the oldest roofed building in Europe *(page 56)*

Es Mercadal · A delightful inland town that specialises in island food – *cuina menorquina (page 51)*

Cala en Turqueta · One of the many lovely little coves in the south of the island *(page 72)*

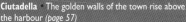

A PERFECT DAY

9.00am Breakfast

Enjoy a typically Menorcan breakfast of fresh orange juice, good coffee and sugar-dusted *ensaimadas* in the Casa de Andalucia in Plaça Reial, near the Parc de'es Freginals.

12 noon Exploring the harbour

Make your way down the broad steps of the Costa de Ses Voltes, stopping to admire the view of the harbour as you go. Once by the port head to S'Abarca (Moll de Levant 21) where Menorcan sandals (*abarcas*) are made on the premises, and choose your favourite colour and design.

11.00am Concert

Go to the Església de Santa Maria in the Plaça de Sa Constitució for the organ concert that takes place daily except Sunday.

1.30pm Lunch

You will be spoiled for choice when choosing where to go for lunch, but elegant La Minerva (Moll de Levant 87, tel: 971 351 995), although expensive, offers an excellent value tasting menu, and the opportunity to eat outside on a floating jetty. Who could ask for more?

10.00am Market in the Claustre del Carme

Visit the morning market in the Claustre del Carme, where glistening fresh fruit and vegetables are piled up beside stalls selling jewellery, household items and some delicious speciality foods.

IN MAÓ

5.00pm Es Castell and Cales Fonts

Once back on dry land, walk to the far end of the harbour and up a small hill, where you can catch a bus to nearby Es Castell. You can explore this pleasant and still very British-influenced little town and then, as the sun goes down, have an early evening drink by the waterside in pretty little Cales Fonts.

3.30pm A boat trip

Take a trip around the harbour in a glass-bottomed boat. A recorded commentary will point out the Illa del Llazaret, which used to be a quarantine centre, the dramatic bulk of the Fortaleza de La Mola, and Golden Farm, wrongly but romantically associated with Lord Nelson and Lady Emma Hamilton.

10.30pm Dinner

After your tour, go to the friendly Siroco restaurant (it's best to book, tel: 971 367 965) back at the harbour for a late dinner – the paella is good – or to sample a wide selection of tapas for which the restaurant is well known.

8.00pm A tour of Castell de Sant Felip

Take a guided tour (in English and Spanish) of the ruins and tunnels of the Castell de Sant Felip, starting at 8.30pm. You will learn a lot about the island's history from the informative guides, and the evening tour is the best and most atmospheric one to take.

CONTENTS

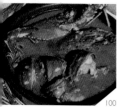

26

100

82

INTRODUCTION

Menorca is an appealing little island. It has neither the dramatic visual appeal of Mallorca's vertiginous coastline nor the brashness of Ibiza's nightlife, but it offers considerable diversity in a very small area – from the rugged, wind-swept stretches of the undeveloped north coast, to the stunningly beautiful bays in the south; plus the pleasures of two handsome, historic cities. All this is what keeps visitors coming back year after year, and the reason that estate agents are flourishing, selling second-home properties to English enthusiasts. In 1993, the island was declared a Unesco Biosphere Reserve – a distinction of which Menorcans are extremely proud. It means that the whole island is under some form of protection, although only S'Albufera d'es Grau is a designated Parc Natural *(see box)*.

Unesco Reserve

A Biosphere Reserve is defined by Unesco as 'a place of important natural and cultural heritage where economic development is compatible with nature conservation'. One of the objectives of the reserve is to control the negative impacts of tourism, which means that no uncontrolled development can take place, although responsible tourism is welcomed.

Geography

Menorca lies just 225km (140 miles) southeast of Barcelona – from where there are regular ferry and air services. It is the second largest of the Balearic group – after Mallorca – but it is still tiny, only 47km (30 miles) from east to west, and some 20km (12 miles) from north to south at its widest point. Roughly 215km (135 miles) of coastline encircle the island, but there

Macarella beach and cove on the island's south coast

is no road to take you all the way around it – you often have to return to the central axis. The island is fairly flat, and the highest point, Monte Toro, crowned by a sanctuary, reaches only 358m (1,170ft).

Landscape and Vegetation

The main road that spans the island, linking the two cities, also roughly divides two distinct geological zones. The northern section is sandstone, with bare rocks and reddish earth; small fields are enclosed by dry-stone walls *(parets seques)*, among which ancient olive trees, myrtle and juniper bushes are rooted, but there is little sign of cultivation. Farming here has always been arduous, and many people abandoned it when tourism offered an alternative. Much of the land in the north of the island is covered by dense scrub known as *maquis*, with heather *(Erica multiflora)* and rosemary *(Rosmarinus officinalis)* present as well.

The southern part of the island is characterised by limestone karst, cut through by lush ravines running down to the sea. The centre is a fertile region of low, gently undulating hills, dotted with neat farmsteads, surrounded by meadows, groves of Aleppo pine, carob trees and stands of holm oak. Few crops, except olives, are produced in any viable quantity, but the dairy industry, introduced by the British *(see page 21)*, still flourishes, and herds of black-and-white cows, which can be seen grazing the fields, provide milk from which to make the local cheese, Queso

Farming is still important in the fertile centre of the island

Lagoon and open sea at S'Albufera d'es Grau

de Mahón, still made in the traditional way *(see page 103)*.

If you visit Menorca in late summer or autumn, you may be struck by the lack of vegetation. But come in spring and you will find large parts of the island covered in wild flowers, including foxgloves, violets and daisies, the spiky-bloomed asphodel and several varieties of wild orchids. Apparently inhospitable areas turn bright yellow with broom, and pink-and-white rock roses bloom well into summer. The evergreen mastic tree *(Pistacia lentiscus)*, from which a rubbery resin, used in making varnish, is extracted, has a reddish bloom.

Birdlife

Menorca is a convenient stopping off point for thousands of migrant birds in spring and autumn, and it also has a diverse resident population. In the marshland areas of the Parc Natural S'Albufera d'es Grau herons and cattle egrets are commonly seen, along with other waders, while booted eagles wheel overhead, and kites and buzzards have their nests along the rocky coast nearby. The Barranc d'Algendar is the place to hear nightingales and see skies filled with alpine swifts; colourful bee-eaters can often be spotted around the coastal dunes.

Climate

Summer temperatures in Menorca average 24°C (76°F) but highs of over 30°C (86°F) are not unusual. Water temperature in mid-summer never drops below 20°C (68°F). Winter months of November to February are the wettest, and the time when the Tramuntana wind blows most fiercely, especially on the north coast. May and September/October, are months of pleasantly warm temperatures and fewer visitors.

Population and Language

The population numbers around 67,000 – about a tenth of Mallorca's total – of which some 22,000 live in the capital, Maó, and a similar number in Ciutadella. These two cities are distinct in character, moulded over the centuries by the different occupying forces: the British in Maó; the Spanish in Ciutadella. Both now make their living chiefly from tourism, as does some 56 percent of the island's population. Strung out between the two cities, a few small, pretty towns retain traditional industries, chiefly the production of leather goods and cheese.

A local woman at Ciutadella's Festa de Sant Joan

Binibeca, a quiet resort consisting mainly of private villas

Menorcans are bilingual in Spanish and Menorquí, a variant of Catalan, which is now the official language. Most people speak Menorquí among themselves, but they all speak Castilian (Spanish), too, and, while they are delighted if foreign visitors know a few words of Menorquí, they don't expect it. Signs and street names are mostly written in Menorquí, although some seem to swerve between the two languages. Some towns have been renamed, and older maps may still give the original, Spanish name.

Getting Around the Island

Most of Menorca's beaches are in the south. Some are tiny, idyllic coves, accessible only on foot through pine woods or by a bumpy car journey over unmade roads. Others are long, broad sweeps of white sand, around which hotels and villa complexes have mushroomed, offering everything visitors need or desire – sometimes at the expense of the area's natural beauty.

As there is no coastal road, drivers have to keep returning to the main central highway (Me-1), on the series of roads that radiate out from it. There is a coastal path, called the Camí de Cavalls (Horses' Way), which was constructed for military patrols in the Middle Ages and which has now been fully renovated and reopened for walkers – with parts of it open to horse riders, too.

Reasons to Visit

Visitors to Menorca – of whom some 58 percent are from the UK, with Germans and Catalans forming the next largest groups – come for a wide variety of reasons. Families with young children appreciate the safe beaches and warm Mediterranean waters and the facilities that have grown up around them but which have not attracted the 'lager lout' tourists that have given Menorca's sister islands a bad name.

The sandy beaches of Menorca are ideal for family holidays

Water sports enthusiasts are attracted by the ideal windsurfing conditions, especially on the north coast around Fornells, and by opportunities for scuba diving in the clear coastal waters.

Walkers love the peaceful paths around the island's coasts and the slightly more challenging ones through the lush central gorges – the *barrancos*, while birdwatchers form flocks of their own during the spring and autumn migratory seasons, especially in S'Albufera des Grau.

Town houses in Ciutadella

Visitors interested in the ancient past delight in the wealth of prehistoric sites – about 1,000 of them – which comprise *talyots* (cylindrical stone watchtowers), *taules* (T-shaped structures probably used for sacrifice and other ritual purposes) and *navetas* (huge, stone-built communal tombs).

Other people come here to explore the historic cities of Maó and Ciutadella, which both have splendid harbours, elegant architecture, atmospheric cobbled streets, some smart shops, a smattering of museums and a plethora of good restaurants. Despite their popularity, these cities have maintained the atmosphere of small friendly towns.

Those who enjoy traditional *fiestas* try to time their visits to coincide with the wild celebrations of the Festes de Gràcia in Maó in early September, or the Festa de Sant Joan in mid-June in Ciutadella *(see pages 96 and 97)*. Come to Menorca and discover which of these varied aspects appeals most to you.

A BRIEF HISTORY

Menorca is an island with a long history. A number of settlers and invaders have taken control and made their mark before being usurped by a more forceful power, and their diverse influences have shaped this small island, leaving lasting monuments and intriguing idiosyncracies.

Prehistoric People

During the Bronze Age, between 3000 and 1300BC, the island was inhabited by people who probably came from the Iberian peninsula. Cave dwellings can be seen in the south – Cales Coves and Cova d'es Colom – and in the north at Cala Morell. Towards the end of this period these early people built *navetes*, so-called because they were shaped like inverted ships (*navis* is Latin for ship). They were communal ossuaries, used to bury bones once the flesh had decomposed in some other (unknown) site. The best known of these is the Naveta d'es Tudons, near Ciutadella *(see page 56)*.

The first settlers were superseded by people of the *Talayotic* culture, named after the stone towers called

Taula at Torralba d'en Salort

talayots built as part of their settlements. Around 200 have survived; among the most spectacular are those at Talati de Dalt, Torre d'en Galmes and Trepucó while the best-preserved settlements are Son Catlar, in the southwest, and Sant Agustí Vell, near Sant Tomás. The other remarkable legacy of the period are the *taules* – T-shaped stone structures composed of two massive stone slabs that are believed to be sites of ritual sacrifice. The most impressive can be seen at the sites mentioned above, and at Torralba d'en Salort and Torre Trencada (*see Where to Go section for details*).

Carthaginians and Romans

Over the centuries, Phoenicians, Carthaginians and Greeks traded with the Balearic Islands and (around 400BC) the Carthaginians gradually colonised them, absorbed them into their trading empire and founded the main ports. The colonisers found that the islanders' skill with stones was not confined to construction work but was also evident in their deadly use of the slingshot. The 'Balearic slingers' were recruited by Hannibal to fight for the Carthaginians in the Punic Wars. The name Balearic probably comes from the Greek word, ballein, meaning 'to throw'.

The Carthaginians were soon superseded as the ruling force: by 123BC the Romans had pacified most of Spain and sent out a force to conquer the islands, which they named Balearis Major (Mallorca) and Balearis Minor (Menorca). They built roads, such as the one that can still be seen at Puig de Santa Agueda, and established ports: Port Magonum (Maó), Jammo (Ciutadella) and Sanisera (Sanitja). Some early Christian basili-

Roman remains

Archaeologists are currently excavating the ruins of the Roman settlement of Sanisera (Sanitja), at Cap de Cavalleria, which has only recently been discovered (*see page 47*).

Remains of the Roman basilica at Son Bou

cas survive from the end of the era, most notably Son Bou and Fornás de Torelló, which has a magnificent paved mosaic.

After the collapse of the Roman Empire, the Balearics were subjected to continuous plundering, chiefly by the Vandals (*c*.AD425) who destroyed most traces of Roman civilisation. The next rulers to give any sense of continuity were the Moors; a Moorish army had landed on the Iberian peninsula in 711 and in just seven years, most of Spain was under Moorish rule. At first the caliphs (rulers) were content simply to accept tribute from Mallorca and Menorca, but local disturbances prompted them to invade and, despite strong resistance, both islands were conquered at the beginning of the 10th century, when they became part of the Caliphate of Córdoba. In *c*.1080 the islands became a separate emirate, under more aggressive rulers. Very little Moorish architecture survived the early 13th-century Christian conquest, but the legacy can be seen and heard in many place names – those with the prefix Al-, such as Alaior, or Bin-, such as Binibecca and Binmel-là.

The Reconquest

Following the recovery of Jerusalem in 1099 it took 400 years of sieges and battles before Christian rulers succeeded in subduing the Moors. The crusades in Spain were aimed at the eviction of the ruling Muslims and the recapture of all Spanish lands. In 1229, a Catalan army led by King Jaume I of Aragón and Catalunya took Mallorca. The Moors who remained were forcibly converted to Christianity, but Jaume proved to be an enlightened ruler. The Moors on Menorca agreed to pay an annual tribute and were left in peace until 1287, when the long and largely beneficial reign of Jaume I was followed by dynastic rivalry, and the brutal Alfonso III of Aragón found a pretext for invasion. The Moors were defeated and expelled or killed. After Alfonso's death, Jaume II, a wiser ruler, stimulated trade in the Balearics. In the 14th century, Menorca's economy prospered, but when trade routes to the East were cut by the Turks in the mid-15th century, things went seriously downhill.

A monument to Alfonso III stands in Maó

The Golden Age

In 1492, the newly unified Spain under the Catholic Monarchs, Ferdinand and Isabella, completed the Reconquest, taking Granada, the only Moorish enclave left on the Iberian peninsula. In the same year, Christopher Columbus, funded by the Spanish Crown, sailed across the Atlantic. Over the subsequent century and a half, known as the Golden Age, Spain imposed its language, culture and religion

Ciutadella's Fort Sant Nicolau, built to deter Turkish raiders

on the Americas, creating a vast empire. Conquistadors extracted vast riches in silver and gold, but, plagued by corruption and incompetence and drained of manpower and ships by such adventurism as the dispatch of the Armada against England in 1588, Spain was unable to defend her interests.

The Balearic Islands did not share in the riches of these years. For them, this was a period of great instability. Along with Catalunya, they were forbidden to trade with the New World, and their existing trade eastwards was interrupted by pirate raids and attacks by the powerful Turkish fleet. These incursions culminated in the devastation of Maó in 1535 and, after a bitter 10-day siege, of Ciutadella, in 1558. The fortress of Sant Felip at the entrance to the port of Maó and the imposing Fort Sant Nicolau in Ciutadella were built in response to these attacks.

Changing Fortunes

The daughter of Ferdinand and Isabella married the heir to the Holy Roman Emperor, Maximilian of Habsburg. The Spanish crown duly passed to the Habsburgs and remained in their hands until the feeble-minded Carlos II died childless in 1700. France seized the chance to install the grandson of Louis XIV on the Spanish throne. A rival Habsburg claimant was supported by Austria and Britain, who feared a powerful Spanish-French alliance. In the subsequent War of the Spanish Succession (1702–13) most of the kingdom of Aragón, including the Balearics, backed the Habsburgs.

Aware of the importance of Maó's harbour, Britain seized Menorca in 1708 and retained it, under the Treaty of Utrecht, once the war was over. One of the most lasting British acts was to make Maó the capital, instead of Ciutadella. Relations with the occupiers were fairly harmonious; under the first British governor, Sir Richard Kane *(see box below)* a road was built to link the two cities, and the economy was improved and strengthened. In 1756, at the beginning of the Seven Years' War, French troops captured the island. They founded the town of Sant Lluís (near Maó), but their occupation was short-lived: under the Treaty of Paris in 1763, Menorca was returned to the British.

In order to repel a further attack, numerous fortifications were built, including the Georgetown garrison, later to become Villa Carlos, now Es Castell. Despite this, in 1781, when Spain was aligned with France, Franco-Spanish troops

Sir Richard Kane

The first British governor of Menorca, Sir Richard Kane (1660–1736), was a resourceful and capable man. He drained marshes, introduced Friesian cattle and new varieties of fruit, stimulated the wine industry and financed the water cistern at Es Mercadel. Most importantly, he commissioned the construction of the first connecting road between Maó and Ciutadella, the Camí d'en Kane, some 16km (10 miles) of which still survive *(see page 51)*. It was largely due to his leadership that relations between the islanders and colonisers were so good during the first period of British rule, and he is still remembered with affection.

landed on Menorca, and the island fell to Spain. During the next few years the Spaniards destroyed the fort of Sant Felip and (in 1795) established the diocese of Menorca, with Ciutadella as its bishopric. The British briefly regained the island in 1798 but, under the Treaty of Amiens in 1802, relinquished it to Spain once and for all.

The economy fell into a poor state during the 19th century, and numerous Menorcans emigrated to Algeria, South America and the US. What commercial success was engendered through the wine industry ended when the phylloxera louse destroyed the island's vines at the end of the century.

Republic and Civil War

The early 20th century in Spain was marked by social and political crises, assassinations and near anarchy, culminating, in 1921, in a coup and the dictatorship of General Primo de Rivera. He fell in 1929, and when elections of 1931 revealed massive anti-royalist feeling, the king followed him into exile. The new Republic was conceived amid an outbreak of strikes and uprisings. In February 1936 the left-wing Popular Front won a majority of seats in the Cortes (parliament), but across Spain localised violence displaced debate.

In July 1936, General Francisco Franco staged a coup, which was supported by the military, monarchists, conservatives, the clergy and the right-wing Falangist Movement. Aligned on the Republican government's side were liberals, socialists, Communists and anarchists. The ensuing Civil War (1936–9) was brutal and bitter, and during the three years it lasted, around one million Spaniards lost their lives.

Sadly, Mallorca and Menorca found themselves on opposite sides. While Mallorca's garrison seized the island for the Nationalists, Menorca declared for the Republic, and stayed with it to the bitter end – it proved to be the last Republican stronghold in Spain.

Tourists on the beach in 1966

Transformation and Democracy

Spain remained on the sidelines during World War II, and, after the dark years of isolation known as the *Noche Negra* (Black Night), began a slow economic recovery, boosted by the growth of the tourism industry.

In the late 1950s and early 1960s northern Europeans began visiting Spain and the Balearic Islands in significant numbers. The first charter plane landed in Menorca in 1953, and within two decades a trickle of visitors had grown to half a million. Throughout Spain, tourism helped transform the impoverished country's economy and landscape, as well as influencing society by introducing liberal ideas. Eager to capitalise, both the government and private interests poured everything into mass tourism, triggering a rash of uncontrolled, indiscriminate building. Mallorca and Ibiza experienced an explosive growth in tourism, but Menorca came more slowly to the industry and remained more low key.

Around a third of the
population live in Ciutadella

When Franco died in 1975, his chosen successor, enthroned as Juan Carlos I, managed a smooth transition to democracy: new freedoms were granted to Spanish regions, whose languages and cultures enjoyed a renaissance. The Balearics obtained a degree of autonomy in 1978 and five years later became an autonomous community.

Menorca Today

In 1986 Spain joined the EEC (now the European Union, or EU), which further boosted the economy. In 1993, Unesco declared Menorca a Biosphere Reserve *(see page 9)*. Over the next decade the economy prospered, but there was increasing concern about accelerating tourist resort development, as well as the high price of land, pushed up by foreign ownership. The island government has taken steps to limit the damage inflicted by mass tourism. Strict building regulations have been imposed and a natural park created to protect the land around S'Albufera d'es Grau. Menorca has learned much from the mistakes made by its neighbours, and most visitors to this lovely island will be pleasantly surprised at how little despoliation there is, and how much of its traditions, culture and natural beauty have been preserved.

The recession that affected most of Europe (and the US) in the first decade of the 21st century meant that tourist numbers dropped and businesses suffered. However, the island government has injected a great deal of money into this vital industry, and it is hoped that Menorca's economy will flourish and visitors will continue to enjoy the island's hospitality.

Historical Landmarks

3000–1300BC Menorca populated by cave dwellers who build *navetes*.

1300–123BC *Talayotic* culture, named after the towers called *talayots*.

400BC Carthaginians conquer and colonise the Balearics.

123BC Romans defeat Carthaginians and name the island Balearis Minor; under Roman rule Christianity is established and towns founded.

848 Moorish Caliphs of Spain quell disturbances in the Balearics and impose Islam; Moorish rule in the Balearics lasts for 300 years.

1229 After Palma de Mallorca falls to the Christian army, Menorca agrees to pay tribute to Aragón.

1285–7 Alfonso III invades Menorca.

1492 Spain united under Ferdinand and Isabella.

1708 Menorca is taken by the British in the War of the Spanish Succession, and held under the Treaty of Utrecht when war ends.

1722 British shift the capital from Ciutadella to Maó.

1756–63 French occupy Menorca until it is handed back to the British under Treaty of Paris.

1781 Franco-Spanish troops take Menorca.

1795 Diocese of Menorca is established, with Ciutadella as its bishopric.

1802 The Treaty of Amiens gives the island to Spain

1936–9 Civil War. Menorca declares for the Republic.

1936–75 Franco's dictatorship, with the early years typified by economic hardship; in the 1960s, tourism starts to bring prosperity.

1975 King Juan Carlos I enthroned after the death of Franco.

1978 Statute of Autonomy. In 1983, Balearic Islands become an autonomous province and Menorquí is restored as official language.

1986 Spain joins European Economic Community (now European Union).

2002 The euro becomes the currency of Spain.

2004 PSOE (Socialist Party) wins election in Spain but right-of-centre Partido Popular (PP) holds power in Balearic Island government.

2007 PP fails to win overall majority. Joana Barceló of the PSOE wins third term as president of the Consell Insular de Menorca.

2011 Elections see the PP win 35 of 59 seats in Balearic government.

WHERE TO GO

Most visitors to Menorca arrive at the neat Sant Climent airport, approximately 5km (3 miles) south of the capital, Maó. Others come by sea from Barcelona to the terminals in Maó or Ciutadella, or hop over from Mallorca on a short ferry trip. Once here, getting round the island is not a problem; hiring a car obviously gives you a greater degree of freedom, but if you are based in either of the two cities, you will be able to use the regular and reliable bus service to reach most points of interest. What is more difficult is travelling between resorts by public transport.

A single busy main road, the Me-1, punctuated by a handful of small towns, runs through gently undulating landscape, linking Maó in the east and Ciutadella in the west – a distance of 47km (30 miles). A network of minor roads lead to the wetlands of S'Albufera d'es Grau and the port of Fornells in the craggy northeast, and to the idyllic coves and long sandy beaches in the south. At present there is no road running all the way round the coast: you must return to the central axis between destinations. Some minor roads are poor but have been improved enormously in recent years.

MAÓ

Maó, the largest town, with a population of around 22,000, is the business and administrative capital of Menorca but above all, it is a port. The 5km (3-mile) long, deep-water natural harbour, guarded by forts and shielded by surrounding hills, caught the eye of the British Navy early in the 18th century. In 1708, during the War of the Spanish Succession,

Ciutadella, the former capital of the island

Three centuries on, Maó's harbour still attracts British visitors

the British seized the island and kept it until 1802, apart from two periods: they relinquished it to the French between 1756 and 1763, and the Spanish held it for 16 years from 1782. The British shifted the capital from Ciutadella to Maó, and built a road between the two. Their occupation left its mark in a number of ways: they introduced gin and the dairy industry to the island, and both have flourished ever since. They also introduced sash windows to Maó – a rare thing in the Mediterranean.

Around the Plaça de s'Esplanada

The streets of the old city are narrow, and many are pedestrianised, so the only way to explore it is on foot. If you drive into town, park in the underground car park (Mon–Sat 8am–11pm) in the large, palm-lined **Plaça de s'Esplanada**, which was formerly used by the British as a parade ground. If you come by bus, you'll be dropped off at the terminus to the west of the square. Old people sit chatting on stone benches, and children clamber and swing in a little playground, but despite some elegant buildings (among which a Burger King has been situated), it is not a particularly remarkable square. An obelisk commemorates those who fell in the Spanish Civil War (1936–9), and soldiers guard the still-operational barracks behind it. As the monument refers only to those who died on the Nationalist side, it is not uncommon to see it embellished with graffiti. On Tuesdays and Saturdays a huge market occupies the centre of the square.

Just off the eastern side of the square, in Carrer Sa Rovellada de Dalt, is the **Ateneu Cientific**, **Leterari i Artístic** (July–Sept Mon–Fri 10am–2pm; check with the tourist office for winter hours; free), an old-fashioned place that is home to Menorca's most important cultural association. It contains a library, and a collection of landscapes, still lifes, ceramic plates and wall tiles. You will have to ask if you want to see the ante-chamber, which is full of stuffed native birds, fish in formalin, seashells and minerals that are kept under lock and key.

The Carrer de Ses Morreres, a busy shopping street with some smart boutiques, runs from the *plaça* towards the old town and the port. A bust commemorates Dr Mateo José Orfila (1787–1853), who was born at No. 13 and went on to found modern toxicology and pathology in the Institut Pasteur in Paris. At the intersection with Carrer de Bastió, where a sinuously curved first-floor window

House of Hanover

Carrer Hannover (the spelling is intentional) was named in honour of the Hanoverian regiment garrisoned in the Plaça de s'Esplanada during the first period of British occupation (1708–56). It is a reminder that during these years the British throne was occupied by members of the House of Hanover.

Festival figures are stored in the town hall

grabs the attention, the street becomes the pedestrianised Carrer Hannover (also called Costa de Sa Plaça; *see box on page 29*).

The Central Plaça

There are more shopping opportunities here, before the road passes through little Plaça de Colón, with a statue of a young girl adorning a fountain, and an excellent bookshop, and you reach the **Plaça de Sa Constitució**, which is dominated by the great **Església de Santa Maria** (daily 7.30am–1pm, 6–8.30pm; free). Founded by Alfonso III shortly after his victory over the Moors in 1287, it was rebuilt in the mid-18th century, when the British controlled the island. It is an eclectic mixture of architectural styles. The facade is neoclassical, the single-aisled nave is pure Catalan Gothic, and the great altar is embellished with Baroque and rococo flourishes. The most renowned object in the church is the mighty organ, with 3,210 pipes; a masterpiece of its kind, it was commissioned from a renowned Swiss organmaker in 1809. Between June and October, half-hour concerts are held from Monday to Saturday at 11am (small entrance fee), and it is lovely to sit and listen to the music swelling around you, while you take time to examine some of the details of the church.

Another imposing building in the square, the **Ajuntament** (Town Hall), was built on the site of a medieval fortress, but very little survives from the earlier structure. The facade is crowned by a bell wall and clock tower, which was donated to the city by the first British governor, Sir Richard Kane *(see page 21)*. The huge male and female figures outside the main council chamber wearing Menorcan folk dress are carried through the streets of Maó during festivals.

Sant Roc and Sant Francesc

Opposite the Town Hall, Carrer de Sant Roc leads to the late 15th-century **Port de Sant Roc**, the only one of Maó's mighty medieval town gates surviving from the original fortifications. In a niche above it is a sculpture of Sant Roc, who is believed to have saved Maó from a plague outbreak. A few yards to the left is the Plaça del Bastió, with restaurants and cafés surrounding a children's play area in the centre.

Turning right from the gate, along Carrer des Rector Mort, through what used to be the smartest suburb of Maó, you reach Carrer d'Isabel II (which you could also have followed from the Town Hall), at the far end of this street you'll come to the Plaça d'es Mon-estir and the **Parròquia de Sant Francesc d'Assís** (daily 10am–noon, 5–7pm, except Thur pm; free). Completed in 1792, after many years' work, this was the church of a Franciscan monastery, founded in the mid-15th century. Although the entrance doorway looks Romanesque, it is in fact

Sant Roc is Maó's only surviving medieval gate

The impressive bulk of Sant Francesc

Renaissance. Inside, a 19th-century *grisaille* wall painting illustrates scenes from the life of St Francis; the Chapel of the Immaculate Conception is decorated in highly ornamental Churrigueresque style.

All that remains of the former monastery is the elegant cloister, which houses the extensive historical and archaeological collections of the **Museu de Menorca** (Apr–Oct Tue–Sat 10am–2pm, 6–8.30pm, Sun 10am–2pm, Nov–Mar Tue–Sat 9.30am–2pm, Sun 10am–2pm; charge). Exhibits range from *talayotic* finds to Greek and Roman amphorae, Islamic tiles, Spanish and British ceramics – the Spanish ones are most attractive – and 20th-century paintings, while modern sculpture is displayed in the courtyard.

Carrer d'Isabel II and Plaça de la Conquista

Retracing your steps along Carrer d'Isabel II you will pass a number of places of interest: a narrow alley leading through whitewashed arches down to the port; the colonial-style palace of the former British governor, today the seat of the Gobierno Militar. You will also pass several smart mansions with Georgian doorways and sash windows, as well as a wonderful candle shop, the Cereria Abella, before arriving back at the Town Hall.

Turn left down the narrow Carrer Alfons II and you will find yourself on the other side of the huge church of Santa Maria, in Plaça de la Conquista. Here, the patrician house called Ca'n Mercadal contains the municipal library, a monument to Alfonso III stands outside the rear entrance to the church, and an interesting shop called Antiguedades Alfonso III, at No. 7, sells antiques and gifts. From the end of a cul-de-sac called Pont d'es Castell there is a fabulous view across the harbour.

Carrer Nou to Claustre del Carme

From Plaça de Sa Constitució, follow Carrer Nou, a bustling, pedestrianised shopping street, to Plaça Reial, a little square packed with café tables, where the Casa de Andalucia makes excellent sandwiches. Going west, up Costa d'en Deià, you come to the arched entrance to the **Parc d'es Freginal** (daily 8am–9pm; free), a city park that offers a shady green refuge from the summer heat, and has a children's play area. It really comes into its own in the days before the Festa de la Vierge de Gràcia (7–9 Sept; *see page 96*), when jazz concerts are held here.

Just around the corner is the well-renovated **Teatre Principal**, in front of which is a large statue of a discus thrower. Italian architect and operatic tenor Giovanni Pelaggi designed the original building, and the curtain first rose here in 1829. Apart from Opera Week (during Semana Santa, the week preceding Easter), little remains of the glorious days of opera, when Italian ensembles began their tours of Spain in Maó, but there is a full programme of performances, including classical concerts, and Latin American music *(see page 95)*.

Going east, from the Plaça Reial, along Carrer Sa Ravaleta, another good shopping street, you will soon come to the huge 18th-century Església del Carme and its adjoining cloister, the **Claustre del Carme**. The cloister was confiscated and deconsecrated in 1835, like most monastic property in Spain, and after serving a number of secular purposes it was transformed into the city market in the 1980s. Alongside fresh produce stalls are others selling speciality foods, jewellery, shoes and gifts. The central courtyard is used for occasional concerts and for outdoor film screenings – known as Cinema a la Fresca. Below ground level, reached by escalator, there is a Spa supermarket. The Café Bar Mirador, with entrances both inside and outside the cloister, has a large sunny terrace with fantastic views over the harbour.

Stopping for a chat outside the Claustre del Carme

What the dispossessed Carmelites would have made of it all, we will never know, but they would probably have been happier with the **Museu Hernández Sanz Hernández Mora** (Mon–Sat 10am–1pm; free), which is also part of the complex. The museum displays the private collections of furniture, paintings, engravings and maps, dating from the 18th to the 20th centuries, which the Hernández family bequeathed to the city.

Two City Squares

Some 50m/yds up the road to the east of the church and cloister you will come to the **Plaça de Miranda**, named after Almirante Augusto Miranda y Godoy, who founded the naval station at Maó in 1916. A bust of the admiral tops a tall plinth in a commanding position above

A daily market is held in the cloister

the harbour, but the square is otherwise somewhat neglected, and dominated by the ramp to an underground car park and the glass structures housing the pedestrian exits.

Back outside the cloister is the **Plaça d'Espanya**, a hub of constant coming and going. In the **Mercat**, the ornate fish market (mornings only), fish and seafood of all kinds are piled high on beds of ice. It is perched on a bastion that was part of the city wall – not the original medieval one, but the Renaissance structure that replaced it.

The Harbour

From here (or from the Portal de Mar running down the side of the Plaça de Sa Constitució), you will reach the gently curving road and broad steps of **Costa de Ses Voltes**, brightened by palm trees and flowering shrubs, that lead to the harbour spread out below. When cruise ships are in port, the area is busy with hair braiders, henna tatooists and stalls selling san-

Es Castell

dals, sunglasses and sarongs. Opposite Ses Voltes, glass-bottomed boats make hour-long trips round the harbour – an excellent way to get your bearings and gain a different perspective on the city *(see box opposite)*.

The huge natural harbour is known simply as **Es Port** and it is still a busy working port as well as a haven for pleasure craft, large and small, and some very luxurious. To the west of Ses Voltes, along the **Moll de Ponent** (meaning Western Quay) is the Zona Pesquera – the area used by the fishing fleet – and the Estació Marítima, the passenger terminal for ferries to mainland Spain and Mallorca. Opposite is a string of restaurants plus a couple of ceramic shops with some interesting pieces, shops selling the ubiquitous Menorcan sandals called *abarcas*, and the island's Pou Nou brand of T-shirts and casual cotton clothes. Past them, and past a splendid but neglected Art Nouveau-style building that was once the headquarters of the island electricity company, is the **Destileria Xoriguer** (Moll de Ponent 93; www.xoriguer.es), which distills and sells the island's gin and a number of brightly coloured herbal and fruit-based liqueurs. You can wander in and try some of the products, but the bottles on sale aren't much cheaper than you will find in other stores.

To the east of Ses Voltes, along the **Moll de Llevant** (Eastern Quay) is another line of restaurants with tables out on the pavement, ships' chandlers, a number of places that hire and repair boats, and one, at No. 21, where *abarcas* are made on the premises to your own requirements *(see page*

91). If you keep walking, you will come to Cala Figuera and a steep hill that leads up to the main Maó–Es Castell road.

Es Castell

From the main road, or from the terminal in Maó, buses run every half hour to **Es Castell**, which is virtually a suburb of Maó. Built on a grid pattern by the British, it was first called Georgetown, and then became Villa Carlos, the name by which it is still known to many local people. The main square,

❷

A Trip Round the Harbour

Taking a boat trip is the best way of appreciating the beauty of the city, which appears to rise straight out of the sea. Glass-bottomed boats, broadcasting a recorded commentary, run from the Ses Voltes area to the mouth of the harbour, where they stop so that passengers can have a look at the seabed from a viewing gallery. The boats go past the **Illa del Rei** (King's Island), where the British built a naval hospital that was used by the Spanish military until the 1960s. They also pass the **Illa Plana** (Flat Island), which was a quarantine site until the Lazareto station was built. You pass through the George Canal, constructed in 1900 to give easier access to steamships, and the forbidding walls of the ex-quarantine hospital on **Illa del Llazteret**. Between 1817 and 1917, some 400,000 people spent time here – some were detained for a quarantine period, while others were treated for a variety of infectious diseases, including yellow fever. Part of the building has been renovated and is now used as a conference centre and a summer holiday resort for social security workers. Ahead of you looms the impressive fortress of **La Mola**, and you can admire **Golden Farm** up on the hill to the north and the smart summer villas edging Cala Llonga. On the south side, you'll see boats at anchor in Cales Fonts and the colonial Collingwood House in Es Castell, which is now the **Hotel del Almirante**, before slipping back into harbour wiser than when you left.

Inside Fort Marlborough

the **Plaça de s'Esplanada** – once a parade ground, like the one of the same name in central Maó – is huge, but has a pleasant neighbourhood atmosphere in the early evening, when people gather at café tables in the centre, and children amuse themselves in a little play park. At one end of the square stands an imposing terracotta-coloured building that is now the police headquarters. It is shared by the offices of the Justice of the Peace and the local radio station, but they have to make do with small side entrances. At the other end of the square, huge cannons stand outside the **Museu Militar** (June–Aug Mon–Fri and the first Sun of month 10am–1pm, Sept–May Mon, Wed, Fri 10am–1pm; charge), home to an interesting collection of militaria.

A short walk from the square down Carrer Stuart brings you to **Cales Fonts**, a pretty harbour lined with fish restaurants that gets very animated at night.

If, instead of dropping down into Es Castell, you continue along the main road, you come to the turning for Sol d'Este, a development so named because this corner of Menorca is the easternmost point, the place where the sun rises first in the morning. A number of bars and restaurants have names like The Rising Sun and El Sol Naciente. Nearby lie the ruins of the **Castell de Sant Felip** (June–Sept guided tours daily 8.30pm, Thur and Sun 10am, Oct–Nov and Mar–May Sat 10am; charge). The night tours are the most atmospheric.

A narrow road leads to **Cala Sant Esteve**, a pretty cove that relative inaccessibility and lack of a beach have enabled to retain its individuality. **Fort Marlborough** (May–Oct Tue–Sat 10am–1pm, 5–8pm, Sun 10am–1pm; charge), an 18th-century British fort with a Martello tower and underground galleries, stages explosions as part of a 45-minute tour.

S'Altra Banda

The road that runs from the west end of Maó's harbour will take you along the port's north side, which locally is called simply **S'Altra Banda** (The Other Side), past the naval base, towards a fine, terracotta manor house, officially called Finca Sant Antoni but usually known as **Golden Farm**. Legend has it that Admiral Horatio Nelson (1758–1805) used it not only as his headquarters but also for romantic trysts with his mistress, Lady Emma Hamilton. In fact, Lord Nelson made only one brief visit to Menorca – and Lady Emma did not come with him.

The road passes the smart suburb and little bay of **Cala Llonga**, before crossing a bleak, inhospitable stretch of land and a narrow causeway to the promontory on which stands the huge **Fortaleza de la Mola** (www.fortalesa lamola.com; May–Sept daily 10am–8pm, Oct 10am–6pm, Nov–Apr Tue–Sun 10am–2pm; charge; guided

Golden Farm has a fine vantage point over the harbour

Fortaleza de la Mola – heavily fortified but never attacked

tours available, extra charge, for reservations tel: 971 364 040). The fort – also known as Fortaleza de Isabel II, after the Spanish queen – was built in the 1830s to replace the castle of Sant Felip, which the Spanish destroyed when they took the island in 1782, at the end of the second period of British occupation. It was highly fortified and given massive gun emplacements, but was never attacked. Your guide (if you have one) may or may not mention that, until as late as 1968, it served as one of Franco's most notorious political prisons.

THE NORTHEAST

The northeast of Menorca is a sparsely inhabited region, much of it protected by the Parc Natural de S'Albufera des Grau. Our route takes in the wetlands and dunes of the park and the village of Es Grau, as well as the remote headland and lighthouse of Favàritx. It then covers a couple of small developments, including Arenal d'en Castell – an example of what not to do when establishing a tourist resort. Next, it takes in the idyllic fishing port of Fornells and the bleak but beautiful Cap de Cavalleria with its fascinating birdlife, before either circling back via country roads to Fornells or returning to Maó along the main road.

   If you are dependent on public transport, you will have to travel using buses from Maó to Es Grau, to Fornells and to Arenal d'en Castell, rather than making the circular trip.

S'Albufera des Grau and Cap de Favàritx

Take the road from Maó signposted to Fornells and after a very short distance turn off right towards Es Grau. The road runs through gently undulating land, with broad cycle tracks on either side, for about 4km (2½ miles), before reaching the well-marked entrance to the **Parc Natural de S'Albufera**. You can get information from the Centre de Recepción Rodríguez Femenias on the main Maó to Es Grau road, Km. 3.5 (www.parquesnaturales.consumer.es; Wed–Sat 9am–6pm, Sun 9am–3pm). There are plenty of clearly marked paths that make for easy walking through the protected land, where olives, juniper and prickly pears give way to Aleppo pines and strong, wiry marram grass, as you approach the dunes surrounding the freshwater lake. Attracted by herons, terns, cormorants and ospreys, birdwatchers love this place, especially during spring and autumn migratory periods.

The protected S'Albufera des Grau

A sombre event

In 1756 Favàritx was the setting for an ignominious incident in British history, when Admiral John Byng, sent to relieve British troops in Maó, became involved in battle with the French and retreated, leaving the island in their hands. Back in England, he was courtmartialled for negligence and executed by firing squad.

The lake is separated from the sea by a narrow strip of beach, which can also be reached by driving another 2km (1 mile) up the road from the park entrance to the unpretentious village of **Es Grau**. Here, whitewashed houses cluster around the harbour and tamarisk grows with its roots almost in the sea. There are a couple of cafés and restaurants on the waterfront, and trips can be taken in summer on glass-bottomed boats out to little Illa d'en Colom and around the estuary.

Return to the main road and after approximately 7km (4 miles) take a right turn to **Cap de Favàritx**, which is also part of the Parc Natural. This once rough and bumpy road has mostly been resurfaced and even given road markings. The landscape through which it runs is bleak and bare, with scant vegetation apart from scrub and succulents. It culminates in a grey slate headland lashed by the fierce Tramuntana wind, where the lighthouse, the **Far de Favàritx** (closed to the public), shines out to sea. The cape has a beauty of its own and is the kind of place that makes you aware of the awesome power of nature.

Northern Resorts

Head back to the Fornells road now, and, if you are wondering what else this corner of the island holds, take a right turn after 7km (4 miles) towards **Port d'Addaia**. Turn right at the roundabout to the port, which is pleasant enough but surrounded by a characterless sprawl of villas and apart-

ments covering the headland between Cala d'Addaia and Cala Molins.

Return to the roundabout and head for **Na Macaret**, which is much nicer, although there's not much going on, and the beach is tiny. There's a pretty harbour, though, with fishermen's cottages clustered around, and ducks swimming on the tranquil waters. Two or three reasonably priced restaurants cater to tourists, some of whom come on the road train from Arenal d'en Castell. The new housing development, mainly summer homes for people from Maó, is restrained and in keeping. In winter, everything closes down.

Back at the roundabout, the third exit leads to **Arenal d'en Castell**, the only place in the north of the island to have been given over completely to mass tourism. The resort is dominated by two huge, ugly hotels, with supermarkets and other facilities, resembling a rather ill-conceived public housing project. Behind them is a dense complex of holiday apartments. The beach, though – a wide horseshoe arc of golden sand, where surfboards, pedaloes and sun loungers can be hired – is splendid and the water is safe and shallow. A snack bar on the beach promises live music nightly, but most

Sleepy Na Macaret, seen from Port d'Addaia

of the evening entertainment takes place in the hotels.

Back to the main road now and head north. If you are looking for a quieter beach, turn off after 3km (1½ miles) to **Son Parc**. Bordering an 18-hole golf course *(see page 88)* this is an up-market, although somewhat featureless, *urbanización,* its rows of holiday apartments and villas all remarkably similar. Its best feature – and the reason for its existence – is the lovely sandy beach, fringed by pinewoods.

Ses Salines and Fornells

The road between Son Parc and the Carretera Maó–Fornells has undergone a facelift, having been entirely resurfaced and widened in places, making this 5km (3-mile) drive through shady pines far more pleasant. The main road then runs around the bay. Just before you get to Fornells, where a turning on the left is signed to Platjes de Fornells, the road leads

Fornells is an idyllic fishing village with some great restaurants

through an elaborate arched gateway to a private 'country club' village. Almost opposite the turning is **Ses Salines**, an exclusive villa complex on the inlet, with a Club Náutic and attached restaurant, a small hotel *(see page 138)* and a strip of beach, usually busy with keen sailors and windsurfers. Windsurf Fornells gives lessons in sailing and water skiing as well as wind-surfing *(see page 83)*.

An idiosyncratic doorway in Fornells

Follow the road along the sheltered inlet, and there's nowhere to go but **Fornells**. This idyllically pretty **5** fishing village is popular with the boating fraternity and with Catalan visitors from Barcelona. It has a number of pleasant hotels and makes a good base for exploring the coast. Fornells still has a working fishing fleet, even if tourism is more of a money spinner these days. A string of restaurants along the harbour sell the catch in various guises and all have their own version of *caldereta de llagosta*, the lobster stew that is Fornells' speciality *(see page 101)* and which King Juan Carlos has been known to order on several occasions, when the royal yacht drops anchor here. Prices are pretty kingly, too, but the stew is delicious. If it's beyond your budget, there are plenty of excellent, less expensive alternatives.

Fornells is a low-key place, bursting with civic pride, its pristine, whitewashed houses decked with gleaming dark-green shutters, narrow streets scented with flowering tobacco plants,

Torre de Fornells

and a modest, unadorned church, Sant Nicolau, with a bell tower.

Beyond the village you can either walk or drive to **Torre de Fornells** (May–Sept Tue–Sun 11am–2pm, 5–8pm; charge) a sturdy fortress built on the windy headland by the British in 1802. The defensive tower has been renovated, and there is a small museum inside concentrating on local and military history. Below the tower, a little shrine, the Ermita de Lourdres is surrounded by candles and flowers, both real and plastic. From this vantage point the headlands, buffeted by the Tramuntana, stretch out on either side of the bay, bleak and desolate.

Cap de Cavalleria

From the crossroads about 3km (2 miles) back down the main road, there is a narrow road to **Cap de Cavalleria**. A short way along, a right turn is signposted to Cala Tirant, an attractive bay, but one that demands a rough and dusty 2km (1-mile) drive, or else a walk. Carry on towards Cap de Cavalleria, which was named after the estates into which Menorca was divided, for logistical purposes, after the Christian reconquest. Continue driving for another 4km (2 miles) or so through wetlands alive with birds, and farmland where sheep and cattle graze, and you will come to a small car park, from where paths lead across hills and dunes to the beach.

Carry on driving, and you will come to the **Ecomuseu de Cap de Cavalleria** (www.ecomuseodecavalleria.com; daily July–Sept 10am–8.30pm, Apr–June and Oct 10am–7pm;

charge), with displays on the history and ecology of the area, and finds from the Roman settlement of Sanitja, which has only recently been discovered. Archaeological digs are continuing, and further finds are being made. Three-week-long archaeological field schools are held here in the summer months. There's a pleasant café, with tables under the pine trees, making it a good place to stop for refreshment.

You can drive to the lighthouse on the tip of the cape, passing the Roman site and the Torre de Sanitja, the Martello tower built by the British in 1798.

Binimel-là and Cala Pregonda

Back down the road, the way you came, there is a turning to the beach of **Binimel-là**, a pretty place where a beach bar operates in summer, and you can sometimes hire pedaloes. The last bit of the road is unmade and pretty rough, so it is advisable to walk the final stretch. If you want to swim at the secluded **Cala Pregonda** just round the coast to the west, you'll definitely have to walk, as there is no road. It's not a taxing walk; the path is unmarked, but as long as you follow the

Birds on the Cape

There is a wealth of birdlife on the drive to Cap de Cavalleria. Buzzards and herons are quite common and can be seen from the road; there are also two rare species, although these are less often seen. One is a type of vulture known as a moixeta (Neophron percnopterus); the other is the Balearic shearwater (Puffinus mauretanicus), belonging to the albatross family group. The shearwaters spend most of their lives at sea but come ashore from February to June to breed and lay their eggs in caves or holes in the ground. There are only 3,000 reproductive pairs in the world, and only one chick from each clutch is raised. The birds leave for Cantabria and the English Channel, and return here in September.

coast you should not go far wrong. It is a beautiful spot, its sandy beach backed by pine woods. Take a picnic, as there are no services or facilities here.

From the cape you can return to Fornells, if that is your base, by retracing your route past the Cavalleria turning. If you are heading back to Maó, continue on the rural road through farmland to Es Mercadal where you join the Me-1, the main highway.

Cala Pregonda

THE CENTRE OF THE ISLAND

The busy main road from Maó to Ciutadella is only 47km (30 miles) long, and, unless you get stuck behind a truck, the direct journey should take less than an hour. This route will make a number of stops, however, as well as offering the option of taking the old road, the Camí d'en Kane. Just outside Maó you can visit the prehistoric sites of Talatí de Dalt and Rafal Rubí before continuing to Alaior, a cheese-making centre, and to the pretty market town of Es Mercadal. Just outside the latter is Monte Toro, the highest point on the island and a major pilgrimage site. Ferreries is the next town on the main road, and a detour can be made from here to Santa Agueda, which is home to the remains of a castle and a Roman road. Just before reaching Ciutadella there are several more prehistoric sites that are worth visiting, in particular the great stone tomb called the Naveta des Tudons.

Talatí de Dalt and Rafal Rubí

Leaving Maó, you pass the monastery church of **Ermita de Gràcia** and the cemetery. The church was built in the late 15th century, and the nave is Gothic, but the striking snow-white facade dates from 1733. Inside, votive offerings give thanks from sailors and fishermen rescued from the seas.

Just 3km (2 miles) outside the capital, a sign points to the **Talatí de Dalt** (daily 10am–7pm; charge Apr–Oct). The settlement is believed to date from the end of the Bronze Age, *c.*1400BC. Surrounded by gnarled olive trees and carobs this atmospheric site includes a large central *talayot*, some burial caves and the remains of several circular houses, but the star piece is a slim *taula* with a leaning column, believed to have come to rest by accident rather than design.

Back on the main road, you will soon see a sign for the **Navetes de Rafal Rubí**, an open site (free) with two collec-

The Bronze Age Talatí de Dalt

Alaior is dominated by its great sandstone church

tive ossuaries, stone structures shaped like upturned boats. Crawl through the low doorway of the better-restored one, to appreciate the spacious interior, over 2m (6½ft) high.

Alaior

The first town along the road is **Alaior** (pop. 6,400), the third-largest on Menorca. Most of the cheese known as Queso de Mahón is made here, not in Maó. A mass of white houses cluster on a low hill, dominated by the sandstone church of **Santa Eulalia** (built 1674–90), with an exuberant Baroque doorway. There are several other impressive buildings, including Can Salort, in narrow Carrer Major, part of the Balearic Islands University. Opposite, the 18th-century Casas Consistoriales (another name for Town Hall) is splendid, especially its elaborate balcony and central staircase.

From the central Plaça del Constitució, Carrer Forn leads down to the former Franciscan **Convent de Sant Diego**, which functioned for some time as a cultural centre but, after a major four-year renovation, opened as a concert auditorium in 2010. Next door, the cloisters have been remodelled as an apartment block, set around an attractive courtyard, the Pati de Sa Lluna – Courtyard of the Moon.

Carry on downhill (Carrer des Banyer) and you will reach **La Payesa** cheese factory, with a retail outlet opposite (Mon–Fri 9am–1pm, 4–7pm). The factory itself cannot be visited. Coingo (hours as above), the other manufacturer, is on the edge of town in Carrer Es Mercadal.

Camí d'en Kane

The old **Camí d'en Kane**, the cross-island route built by the British in the early 18th century, leads past Alaior's cemetery, about 1.5km (1 mile) north of town. You can pick up the whole surviving stretch, from Maó to Es Mercadal, from a turning 2km (1 mile) along the road from Maó to Fornells. The narrow *camí* runs though gentle countryside, with drystone walls, some crumbling, some topped off with white-painted cement to keep them together. Every so often you pass one of the typical Menorcan olive-wood gates, and an occasional grand *finca*, but few crops are grown along the way, and the road is more interesting historically than scenically.

Steps up to the cistern built by Sir Richard Kane (*see page 52*)

Es Mercadal

If you are continuing west from Alaior on the main road, your next stop will be **Es Mercadal** (pop. 2,400), about 13km (8 miles) further

The statue of Christ on the summit of Monte Toro

on, and a good starting point for hikes through the surrounding countryside. Clustered at the foot of Monte Toro *(see opposite)* this is a sleepy old town of narrow streets and blindingly-white houses, smothered with bougainvillaea blooms in summer. There's a pretty red-tiled *plaça* surrounding the **Església Paroquial de Sant Martin** (usually open for mass only), and stone bridges span the (mostly dry) river bed that skirts the town.

The lack of water in the stream makes it clear why one historical structure came to be built. The cistern, or *aljub*, was the brainwave of governor Richard Kane in 1733. Noting a connection between the shortage of water and frequent outbreaks of disease, he financed the project – a move that was more innovative than it sounds, at a time when the link between water, sanitation and health was little understood. The cistern, which holds 273,000 litres (54,600 gallons), works by collecting and storing the rain that falls on to a flat roof. From the road, all you can see is a narrow flight of steps up to a wooden gate that seems to lead nowhere.

The town's other claim to fame is that it plays host to several restaurants, specialising in authentic *cuina menorquina*. All are good, and one is excellent *(see page 113)*.

Monte Toro

At the eastern entrance to Es Mercadal is the clearly marked road to **Monte Toro**. This is Menorca's highest point, at 358m ◀ **10** (1,170ft); the road up is sinuous but excellent, and the view from the top is splendid.

There has been a shrine here since the 13th century when, according to legend, a bull led a group of monks to a statue of the virgin hidden in the rocks. As bull is *toro* in Spanish, it is easy to see how this story evolved, but the name most likely comes from the Arabic *al-tor*, meaning 'high place'. In the 17th century Augustinian monks built a sanctuary here and stayed till 1835, when monastic property was confiscated. Their church (daily 7am–7pm) was desecrated a century later during the Spanish Civil War, and most of what you see today, including the gaudy, Baroque-style altar, is the result of 1940s' renovation. The courtyard outside is a pleasant place, with a small fountain and lots of glossy plants, and it's a popular spot for visitors to take photographs.

There is still a functioning convent here, and the nuns run the souvenir shop. It shares its hilltop home with the remains of a fort, built in anticipation of a Turkish invasion, a huge statue of Christ, commemorating those who died in an ill-advised Moroccan war in the 1920s, and is completely dwarfed by radar towers that are part of an army post.

The Verge del Monte Toro

The story above is not the only one connected to the statue of the Verge del Monte Toro. According to another local (more believable) tale, when the church was desecrated in 1936, a local man called Joan Albalat saved the figurine from the approaching flames and gave it to farmers at nearby Rafal des Frares to hide until the end of the Civil War. The container in which they buried it is displayed in a side chapel of the church.

In the café here you can get great sandwiches, which can be eaten on a sunny terrace, and there's a restaurant that does a reasonable *menú del dia*.

Sa Farinera and Ferreries

Sa Farinera (daily 10am–noon; free), a converted manor house and mill just outside Ferreries, claims to be an ethnological museum and to sell local products, but is a bit of a let down. The children's playground and small go-kart track will please little ones, but most of the complex is just one huge souvenir shop, plus a restaurant.

A glistening altarpiece in the church of Sant Bartomeu

The fifth-largest town on the island, **Ferreries** (pop. 3,700), is also the highest, at 142m (465ft) above sea level, but is less picturesque than Alaior or Es Mercadal. The old centre, with narrow streets and the parish church of Sant Bartomeu, is attractive, but the town is dominated by streets of newish apartment blocks and an industrial area. However, this does mean that there is plenty of employment in Ferreries, mainly in the thriving shoe industry, so the town is prosperous and does not have to depend on tourism.

Since it is so well situated for walks through the hills to the north and the lush ravines of the south, the town is increasingly geared up to *tur-isme rural*, and in Carrer Mallorca there is a small **Museu de la Natura** (www. gobmenorca.com/cnatura: tel: 971 374 505; hours vary depending on exhibitions so call or check website; free), which focuses on environmental issues. On Saturday morning farm produce and craft items are sold in a large market in the modern Plaça d'Espanya.

Puig de Santa Agueda

About 3km (1½ miles) west of Ferreries is the turning to Binisues and **Puig de Santa Agueda** (264m/866ft), the third-highest peak on the island. It's about an hour's walk from the abandoned school at Binisues, up a steep path through a grove of cork oak to a remarkably well-preserved section of Roman path. On the summit are the ruins of the Castell de Santa Agueda, a fort dating from the Moorish period. There isn't much left, but the view is spectacular.

Talayots and Taules

Back along the main road to Ciutadella, near the Km 37 sign, just after you pass a strange mock castle on your right (Castillo Menorca, a shopping centre with children's playground), there is an inconspicuous pink sign for Torrellafuda on the left. About 1km (½ mile) down a bumpy lane you come to the well-preserved *talayot* and *taula* of **Torrellafuda** (open site; free), beautifully set in a copse of holm oaks.

Although the lovely settlement of **Torre Trencada** (Apr–Oct daily 8am–9pm, Nov–Mar 8am–6pm; free) is just 1km

The remarkable Naveta d'es Tudons

(½ mile) away as the crow flies, to reach it you have to return to the main road, then turn left 2km (1 mile) further on. At first the road is asphalted, but when you reach the Camí Vell it becomes rough and potholed, running between crumbling dry-stone walls (go left at the fork). A five-minute walk through farmland from the car park brings you to an outstanding *taula*, which, unusually, is supported by two other pillars rather than one. The walls surrounding the settlement have all but disappeared, but there is a *talayot* and several burial caves, which are thought to be medieval rather than prehistoric. The site is popular, and people often come here to picnic among the trees. Nearby, in an abandoned quarry, S'Hostal (www.lithica.es) is a stone labyrinth and sculpture garden.

Naveta d'es Tudons

About 1km (½ mile) along the main road, the **Naveta d'es Tudons** (Tue–Sat 9.15am–8.30pm, Sun–Mon 9.30am–3pm; charge) is clearly signed, with a left filter and a large car park, for this Bronze Age burial chamber is one of the most famous prehistoric monuments in Menorca. It stands alone in the middle of a field and has a magical atmosphere – as long as you don't arrive at the same time as a tour bus on a flying visit. During excavations in the 1950s, the remains of about 100 people were discovered in this two-storey ossuary, along with personal effects of bone and bronze. The boat-shaped *naveta* is believed to be the oldest roofed building in Europe.

CIUTADELLA

Menorca's second city, **Ciutadella**, has elegant manorial houses, grand churches, narrow cobbled streets and a friendly, lived-in atmosphere. As Medina Minurka it was the Moorish capital of the island, and, when Alfonso III of Aragón entered the city in 1287, it became the Christian capital. A Turkish army destroyed most of the town in 1558, following a 10-day siege. It was rebuilt, but in 1722 the British gave the status of capital to Maó, because Ciutadella's narrow inlet simply could not compete with Maó's harbour. However, in terms of its natural beauty and choice seafood restaurants, Es Port is hard to beat today.

Although Ciutadella means Little City it has a population of 21,000, only slightly lower than that of Maó. As well as exploring the town and port, this route takes a trip to the

The golden walls of Ciutadella rise above the harbour

northwest corner of the island, to the lovely bay and ancient caves of Cala Morell and the beach at Algaiarens. Buses run three times a day from Plaça dels Pins, but a car obviously gives you more flexibility.

The Harbour

A ▶ Ciutadella's harbour, **Es Port**, is a delight – the archetypal Mediterranean harbour. If you arrive by sea, you will be bowled over by the setting: the ochre-coloured city walls and the fortified structure of the former town hall rising behind them. The long narrow inlet is full of yachts, easily outnumbering the fishing boats, and the quays are lined with cafés and restaurants whose tables reach almost to the water's edge.

You can walk along the Camí de Baix (Lower Road) then take steps up to **Passeig de Sant Nicolau**, which runs past the Club Náutic and gives views of elegant summer homes set in gardens on the far side. Continue to the **Castell de Sant Nicolau** (Tue–Sat 10am–1pm, 6–8pm; free) a sturdy octagonal tower with a small, rather uninspiring museum inside. This is, however, a great place from

The Useful Side of the Harbour

The far side of Ciutadella's harbour, connected by a pedestrian bridge, is less busy and interesting than the near one, but it offers a number of useful services. It is here that you can purchase tickets for the car and passenger ferries to Mallorca, and where you will disembark if you arrive by sea. Boat trips to Platja de Son Saura and Cala en Turqueta on the south coast also start here. As well as a couple of restaurants with excellent harbour views, there are the offices of car-hire companies, and outlets that rent boats and jet skis and organise fishing trips. Further along the quay are busy boat yards, where the activity reminds us that Ciutadella is still a working port.

which to watch the sunset. Outside, a bust commemorates David Glasgow Farragut (1801–70), the son of a local man who emigrated to the US. Farragut became the first four-star admiral of the US and was given a hero's welcome when he visited Ciutadella in 1867.

At the tower, the broad, palm-lined promenade changes its name to Passeig Marítim and continues round the headland as far as little Cala des Degollador, where the road to the southern resorts begins at a roundabout.

Plaça d'es Born

Back on the quayside, the sloping Baixada Caplonc leads up past souvenir stalls and shops to the ceremonial

B ▸ square, **Plaça d'es Born**, its grandeur somewhat marred by a plethora of parked cars. The square is dominated in the centre by a large obelisk commemorating those who died defending the town against the Turks in 1558. A market is held here on Friday and Saturday, and on 23–24 June it is the main site of the Festa de Sant Joan *(see page 96)*, when horsemen ride among the crowds, their steeds prancing and circling on their hind legs.

Most of the buildings in the square date from the early 19th century. Dominat-

The old Ajuntament building in the Plaça d'es Born

ing the west end is the grand, crenellated, former Town Hall – now the police headquarters but still referred to as the Ajuntament – with a colourful mosaic on the ground outside. The sounds emanating from a primary school in the building next door typify Ciutadella's pleasing mix of historical and modern, majestic and mundane. Along the north side, the Teatre Principal, restored after years of neglect, serves as both theatre and cinema. Next door, the Cercle Artístic was once home to an artists' association but is now merely a café, with good harbour views from the back.

In the southeast corner, beside the post office, stands the great bulk of the Església Sant Francesc (open only for mass). It is a mixture of styles as it originated in the late 13th century, was burned by the Turks in 1558, rebuilt, augmented in the 18th and 19th century and desecrated in the Civil War.

The east side of the square is lined with elegant, but somewhat run-down mansions, built for aristocratic families whose descendants, mostly based in Barcelona or Madrid, come for visits in summer. The ground floors have been converted into cafés and souvenir shops – there is even a Burger King. The **Palau de Torresaura** has a splendid portal, a magnificent inner courtyard and Renaissance-style *putti* on the roof. The noble facade of the Palau Vivó is decorated with oriel windows and balconies, and the atrium contains a magnificent double staircase.

People-watching, Plaça d'es Born

Palau Salort
The only one of these grand palaces that can be visited (apart from the Palau Saura

The Palau de Torresaura

which is now an exhibition space) is the neoclassical **Palau** ◀ C
Salort (May–Oct daily 10am–2pm; charge; entrance via the
side door in Carrer Major del Born). Built in 1600 for the
Salort family, it was purchased by Pedro Martorell y Olives,
who redesigned it in 1813, modelling its facade on that of
La Llotja, the Barcelona Stock Exchange. It is well worth a
visit. You buy your ticket in the courtyard from a kiosk that
resembles a Punch and Judy stall, before exploring the
rooms: a kitchen with a vast tiled stove running almost the
length of one wall; the children's bedroom, with a cradle and
a pram; a well-stocked library, a salon with family portraits,
and a dining room, with a table laid for dinner.

Plaça de la Catedral

Carrer Major del Born leads to the **Plaça de la Catedral**,
where street entertainers amuse the crowds and the tourist office *(see page 132)* is housed in the imposing Consell Insular

D building opposite the **Catedral de Santa Maria** (daily 9am–1pm, 6.30–9pm; free). Built of honey-coloured sandstone, it was begun in the early 14th century on the site of an earlier mosque but desecrated by the Turks in 1558. It was damaged by fire during the following century, but was well renovated and in 1795 was elevated to the status of a cathedral, when a papal edict restored the bishopric of Menorca (there had been one back in the 5th century).

The main facade and splendid doorway are in the 19th-century neoclassical style, but the broad nave is Catalan Gothic, as is the great marble altar, covered by an ornate *baldachino*. The Port de la Llum (Door of Light), damaged in the Civil War and subsequently restored, retains its 14th-century ornamentation – magnificent, fabled creatures and coats of arms. Organ concerts (small fee) are held daily at 11.30am throughout the summer, providing a good opportunity not only to listen to the soaring music but also to appreciate the effects of the light filtering through the stained-glass windows.

Catedral de Santa Maria

The quiet inner courtyard of the 18th-century **Palau Episcopal** (Mon–Sat 9am–noon; free) in the Carrer de Cal Bisbe connects the palace and the cathedral. The rest of the palace is closed to the public.

Churches and Mansions

If you take the narrow Carrer del Roser opposite the main door of the cathedral, you will come to the intricate and beautiful doorway of the 17th-century **Es Roser** (Mon–Sat 11am–1pm, 6–9pm; free). Once a parish church, it has had many uses since its desecration in the Civil War. Now renovated by the town council, it serves as an exhibition centre. Its light, airy central hall, the Sala Municipal, hosts temporary exhibitions of modern art.

Just around the corner, next to La Guitarra restaurant (see page 110) is another historic building that has become a venue for art and photographic exhibitions: the **Palau Saura** (Mon–Sat 10am–1pm, 6–9pm when there are exhibitions; free), whose renovation was also largely funded by the town council. The exterior of the palace looks particularly lovely at night, when the overhanging eaves and the arches of the upper storey are illuminated, and the light picks out the intricate details. Many of the buildings in Ciutadella's old town are lit at night, or else gently illuminated by the old-fashioned street lamps; they glow like gold in the narrow streets that fall quiet when visitors return to the resorts at the end of a day's visit.

Almost opposite Palau Saura is another splendid building, the **Palau Martorell**. It is closed to the public, but take a peek inside the great door if it is open, as it often is, for a glimpse of the sumptuous interior.

Restoring the Past

Continuing to the left along Carrer del Santíssím and into Carrer des Seminari, you reach the 17th-century **Convent i Església del Socors**, originally an Augustinian monastery. Most of the building is closed to the public, but summer concerts are held in the pretty cloister, planted with lemon trees, and the ground floor houses the **Museu Diocesà** (May–Oct

Fish stall at the market

Tue–Sat 10.30am–1.30pm; charge). As well as ecclesiastical items, its displays include interesting archaeological finds and a collection of landscape paintings by Pere Daura (1896–1976), who was born in Ciutadella.

On the next corner stands the baronial **Can Saura** where renovation work has temporarily halted (check with the tourist office when you visit). At the back of the building is a centre for the elderly. Also in Carrer des Seminari, on the corner of Carrer Sant Crist, is **Església de Sant Crist** (daily 9am–1pm, 5–9pm; free), built in 1661. Above the altar of this tiny, simple church is a powerful crucifixion figure, restored in 2006, which is deeply venerated because drops of perspiration are said to have appeared on it in the late 17th century.

The Market and Ses Voltes

Now make a detour down Carrer Sant Crist and turn right towards Plaça Françesc Netto and the adjoining Plaça de la Libertat, an attractive arcaded square where the **Mercat** (market) is held on Tuesday to Saturday mornings. Mountains of fruit, vegetables and meat are on sale in the green-and-white-tiled market hall, while fish is available from numerous stalls in the 19th-century pavilion. Bars around the squares do a brisk trade when the market is open.

Retrace your steps to the corner of Carrer des Seminari, and you emerge into a *plaça* and a street that is officially called Carrer de Josep Maria Quadrado, but is always known simply as **Ses Voltes**. Café tables are set out in the centre of the square, which is framed by whitewashed arches, and the shady arcades continue up the street, where, among the gift shops, there is an appetising *confitería* (pastry shop) selling huge *ensaimadas*, and a shoe shop specialising in stylish *abarcas (see page 91)*.

Plaça Nova and Plaça de Ses Palmeres

The road ends in another attractive square full of café tables, **Plaça Nova**. Here the busy, pedestrianised shopping street of Camí de Maó runs to Plaça Alfons III, widely known as **Plaça de Ses Palmeres** (Square of the Palm Trees). This is the eastern edge of town and it marks the spot where the road from Maó reached the old city gates. Traffic roars along the Avinguda de la Constitució on the far side but the square

Café tables invite you to take a break in the Plaça Nova

itself has been paved and pedestrianised, brightened with flowers and lined on two sides by cafés and restaurants.

The white windmill on the other side of the avenue is the **Molí d'es Comtes**, built in the late 18th century and one of the few windmills still standing on the island. There is a bar and shop on the ground floor, and an adjoining restaurant serves good grilled meats.

The Bastió de Sa Font

Go back to Ses Voltes now and take a right turn down Carrer de Santa Clara. You will pass the Monestir de Santa Clara. Continue straight along the narrow road ahead and you reach the stocky **Bastió de Sa Font**, a great bastion built in the late 17th century as part of Ciutadella's fortifications. It now houses the **Museu Municipal** (May–Sept Tue–Sat 10am–2pm, 6–9pm, Oct–Apr 10am–2pm; charge).

Bronze Age and Roman items in the Museu Municipal

The vaulted galleries of this excellent museum house Bronze Age skulls, weapons and domestic utensils from the talayotic period and Roman coins, jewellery and oil lamps, all of which are very well displayed. Some of the finds come from the caves at Cala Morell (see page 68).

Early surgery

Some of the skulls in the Museu Municipal show signs of trepanning, a gruesome method used in cranial surgery. Remarkably, some show wounds that have healed, proving that the patients must have survived.

Completing the Tour

Walk back along Carrer de sa Muradela, overlooking a dry river bed where little flower and vegetable gardens have been cultivated, and you will soon be back at the harbour and Plaça des Born, having almost completed a tour of the city. Before you leave, turn left up Carrer Pere Caplonc into Carrer Sant Rafel, to the delightful **Casa-Museu del Pintor Torrent** (June–Oct Mon–Sat 11am–1pm, 7.30–9.30pm, Sun 8–9.30pm; Nov–Apr pre-arranged visits only, tel: 626 558 126; free), a gallery devoted to the work of the eponymous painter, known as 'the Menorcan Van Gogh', who was born in Ciutadella in 1904. Unlike many provincial artists, who head for the cultural centres of Europe, Torrent spent his life here. His style is somewhat eclectic, but some of his figurative painting is pleasing.

If you are catching a bus from Ciutadella to your next destination, cross Plaça des Born to **Plaça de s'Esplanada**, also known as Plaça des Pins, after the pine trees dotted around the shady square. There are kiosks selling sweets, cafés with outdoor tables, and a children's playground. It has a nice, neighbourly feel to it, especially in the evening, when you are likely to see more local people than tourists.

Cala Morell

Cala Morell and Platjes d'Algaiarens

Just to the north of Ciutadella lies a cluster of tourist resorts, with all the usual facilities, and where most of the accommodation is block-booked by tour companies; these include Cala en Blanes, Cala en Forcat and Los Delfinos. The two most interesting places are Cala Morell and Platjes d'Algaiarens.

Cala Morell, some 9km **⬅15** (5½ miles) from Ciutadella is one of the few places on the northwest coast where development has been permitted – and this only because it was largely done before the more stringent laws came into effect. It is a very up-market development, however, with gleaming white villas set in spacious gardens, surrounded by pines, and a network of broad, well-lit roads.

As you enter the complex, take the left turn at the roundabout with a model *talayot* in the centre. This leads both to a pebbly beach, set in a stunning cove and popular with snorkellers, and a complex of 14 Bronze and Iron Age caves, the **Necrópolis de Cala Morell** (open site; free). Set in the rocks right beside the road, the caves are extraordinary, with niches, chimneys and wall carvings, and their roofs supported by central pillars. It is believed that the caves were used as dwellings as well as for tombs, or ossuaries.

Go back the way you came and after about 3km (2 miles) a signed-posted road (potholed but adequate) leads through farmland and some beautiful pinewoods to the fine, sandy **Platjes d'Algaiarens**, where twin beaches are set in a horseshoe-shaped bay. The bays and beaches are all privately owned and, in summer, to keep numbers down, a guardian at the gate charges €5 per car if you want to drive down the final 1km (½ mile). However, it's a very beautiful spot and well worth the fee if you want to spend a couple of hours or more here. You are welcome to walk down without paying.

THE SOUTH OF THE ISLAND

This route runs from Ciutadella to Maó, taking in the major resorts and beaches of Cala Santa Galdana, Son Bou and Cala N'Porter and a number of lovely little coves, some accessible only on foot or by rough tracks (just accessible by car). It includes the fertile Barranc d'Algendar; Son Catlar and Torre d'en Gaumés, the two best-preserved prehistoric settlements on the island; and the sleepy town of Es Migjorn Gran. To the southeast are the funerary caves of Cales Coves; the architect-designed 'fishermen's village' of Binibeca Vell, and Sant Lluís, a small town founded by the French. The distance would be small if there were a coast road, but you have to keep returning to the Me-1. However, these detours involve some attractive drives and the opportunity to make discoveries en route.

The dramatic Cova d'en Xoroi at Cala N'Porter (see page 78)

The Southwest Corner

Leaving Ciutadella from the roundabout at the end of the Passeig Marítim, a road runs straight down the coast, linking a number of somewhat featureless, sprawling resorts. The best of them is **Cala Blanca** (about 4km/2½ miles from the city) with pine-lined streets and a small sandy beach, although the huge Hotel Mediterrani that looms up as you approach is rather off-putting. Another 5km (3 miles) through flat, rocky landscape brings you to the island's southwest point, **Cap d'Artruix**. Apart from the lighthouse and a line of rather drab villas, there's little to see, but visitors on hired bikes can take full advantage of the flat terrain, and a small road train links the windy cape with the nearby resorts. The nicest of these are **Son Xoriguer** and **Cala en Bosc** – the latter has an attractive new marina and is very popular with the boating crowd as well as with families.

Son Catlar

Back to Ciutadella now, where you should take a right turn at the roundabout on to a road signposted to Sant Joan de Missa and Cala en Turqueta and marked Camí Rural. Rural it certainly is, and you may be surprised, so close to the city centre, to see chickens wandering in the road. When you reach the Son Vivó farmhouse – an imposing building with its name in large letters – take the right fork down a narrow, potholed road for about 5km (3 miles) to **Son Catlar** (daily 10am–9pm or sunset; charge in summer), one of Menorca's most important monuments.

Still enclosed by its original, 1km (½-mile) long perimeter wall, Son Catlar is the largest preserved prehistoric settlement in the Balearic Islands. Established *c*.1400BC, it probably reached its heyday around the 3rd century BC, and was abandoned at the end of the Roman period. There is a splendid doorway in the wall, and within the enclosed area five

Son Catlar: the largest ancient settlement in the Balearics

talayots and a *taula* can easily be seen. One of the special features of the site is the *hypogaeum*, a small underground chamber that was used for funerary purposes. There is a large car park, an information kiosk and public toilets. Take insect repellent, as flies can sometimes be an irritation.

Sant Joan and Cala en Turqueta

Go back to the Son Vivó fork now, and it's around 2km (1 mile) down a bumpy road to the **Ermita de Sant Joan de Missa** (Mon 4–7pm; free), a compact, whitewashed chapel, festooned with vines and with a double-bell wall. It's a peaceful, pretty place but, owing to the limited opening times, most people only see it from the outside. Beyond the chapel to the left, a track branches off to the left towards Cala Macarella, but it's in extremely poor condition. If you want to visit Macarella beach, it's better to go to Cala Santa Galdana *(see page 72)* and walk along the clifftop.

Cala en Turqueta is popular, despite being hard to access

17 ▶ Take the right fork, instead, signed to **Cala en Turqueta**, and after a short distance you come to another right turn, with a 'Welcome' sign and a kiosk where a caretaker ensures that no more than 120 cars take the rough and rocky track down to the car park. You could walk down – it's only about 1.5km (1 mile) – although passing cars throw up quite a lot of dust. It's a lovely cove with clear turquoise waters and walks over the headland through pines and juniper bushes. If you are lucky, you may see a brightly coloured hoopoe, or hear its distinctive call. There are few facilities at the beach, but ice creams and cold drinks are on sale in summer, and there are rudimentary portaloos.

Cala Santa Galdana

Back to the main Me-1 now and, after approximately 16km (10 miles), just before you reach Ferreries, take the turning **18** ▶ to **Cala Santa Galdana**. This is a good, well-surfaced road, passing neat, white-painted cottages and well-tended vegetable gardens, which soon give way to fragrant pine woods. On the 7km (4-mile) drive you also pass two equestrian centres advertising evening shows, and the S'Atalaia camping site *(see pages 90 and 117)*.

Cala Santa Galdana is a salutary example of tourist development let loose on a perfect spot. Pine-studded cliffs drop down to a sheltered bay with sparkling waters and sand so white that it looks almost unreal. As if this wasn't enough, the **Barranc d'Algendar** *(see box on page 74)* cuts through the cliffs here, its stream widening out into a broad, rush-lined river as it reaches the sea.

Back in the early 1970s, this spot proved irresistible, and the developers moved in. Now, three large hotels dominate the small bay, and the Passeig Marítim, parallelling the river, is lined with restaurants and pizzerias, where tomato ketchup on the tables comes as standard. But let's not be churlish: the resort has everything you could ask for in terms of an active holiday – biking, hiking and pony trekking, as well as diving and fishing. It caters well for families, too; the waters are safe and shallow and there's a well-equipped children's playground right in the town centre.

As you drive in, over a narrow bridge, there is a large car park on your right; if it's full, as it may well be in high summer, you shouldn't have to drive far along the Passeig Marítim to find a space. From here you can wander along the commercial strip, past the villas that are part of the Hotel Cala Galdana complex, and the boats bobbing in the marina, where the mouth of the river separates the main resort from the beach. There's a narrow pedestrian bridge across it, which leads to the Restaurant El Mirador, set on a little promontory. The views are absolutely gorgeous, so it's worth stopping for a drink, but the food is only average for its price and service does not always come with a smile.

Cala Macarella and Cala Mitjana

Another advantage of Cala Santa Galdana is that there are two lovely little beaches in unspoiled coves within easy walking distance, and one a little further afield. From the road beside Hotel Audax (wooden steps lead from the back of a small car park) you can walk through pine woods to **Cala Macarella** in about 30 to 40 minutes. Lack of vehicle access helps keep numbers down in this lovely little bay, flanked by cliffs, but it is far from deserted. The sand is fine, the water clear, and a small bar provides refreshments and shower facilities, in summer.

If you feel up to a somewhat longer walk, tiny **Cala Macarelleta**, around the next headland, is more secluded, and therefore popular with nude sunbathers.

From the other side of Cala Santa Galdana, behind the monolithic Hotel Sol Gavilanes (and another car park) a path leads through stone-scattered woodland, redolent with the smell of pines, to **Cala Mitjana**, an idyllic little cove with crystal-clear waters and huge caves in the cliffs. There are no

Barranc d'Algendar

The Barranc d'Algendar runs for about 6km (4 miles) from just west of Ferreries to Cala Santa Galdana. It's the most dramatic and probably the most beautiful of Menorca's limestone gorges. The vegetation is varied, ranging from pines and fruit trees to lush, almost subtropical foliage, while thick reeds and rushes border the river at the Santa Galdana end – unusually, the stream through the gorge runs with water all year round. Butterflies follow you on your way and a wealth of birdlife includes buzzards, kestrels and kites. An individual walker will be faced with a moral decision when reaching gates marked 'Propiedad Privada' (Private Property), but access problems are smoothed out if you go on an organised hike, which can be arranged in Cala Santa Galdana (see page 86).

The cemetery at Es Migjorn Gran

facilities here, so bring supplies if you are coming for the day; the easy walk takes less than 20 minutes, so it is not far to carry a picnic and a beach mat.

If you continue along the road behind the Sol Gavilanes, through quiet streets lined with smart villas set in colourful flowery gardens, you will find a number of places marked 'Mirador', where viewing platforms give stupendous views over the bay.

Es Migjorn Gran, Sant Tomàs and Son Bou

Head back to Ferreries now, and turn right just before you enter the town. The curvy road runs 6km (4 miles) through lush, fertile landscape, limestone rock faces and well-cultivated terraces to **Es Migjorn Gran**. This sleepy town, built by the Spanish in the 18th century, has a meandering Carrer Major, lined with spick-and-span, dark-shuttered houses. There is not much here to detain you but, as well

The beach at Son Bou

as being the starting point for an energetic walk down the Barranc de Binigaus to the sea (about 5km/3 miles each way), it also has one of the best restaurants on the island, **58, S'Engolidor** *(see page 113)*.

It's only about 5km (3 miles) down the road from the town to **Sant Tomàs**, a pleasant but undistinguished resort that originally grew up here because the beaches were long, broad and splendid. They have been helped by a bit of artifice in recent years, however: in 1989 a freak storm made off with all the sand and the crisp white powder you walk through today had to be imported.

The beaches of Sant Tomàs almost meet up with those of the next resort, **Son Bou**. You can walk along, but to reach it by road you have to go back to the main road. You enter Son Bou through a dramatic arch in the rocks and immediately ahead, where you should have a view of the sea, is the bulk of the huge Hotel Sol Pinguinos Milanos. The resort is a sprawling one, but the pristine dunes and beach are now under a protection order (like much of the coast). No more development along the water's edge has been permitted and other new buildings here have been limited to four storeys. A couple of inoffensive snack bars cater to visitors, and pedaloes and sun loungers are for hire. A little road train takes visitors from their hotels down to the beach.

If you walk to the left, past the Sol Pinguinos Milanos on one side of the road and ranks of apartments on the other, you will reach the remains of the 5th-century **Basílica Paleocristiana** which was not discovered until 1951. The entrance gate is usually shut but there is a good view of the beach-side settlement from over a low boundary wall.

Talayotic Sites

On your way back to the main road at Alaior, take a right turn down a well-surfaced road to **Torre d'en Gaumés** ◀ ㉑ (Tue–Sat 9.15am–8pm, Sun–Mon 9.15am–3pm; charge except on Sun), which is the second largest of Menorca's prehistoric settlements. Believed to date in part from the pre-*talayotic* era, it has three *talayots*, a *taula*, circular dwellings, a hypostyle (the name for a hall with supporting columns), and caves and cisterns carved out of the soft sandstone rock.

Yet another megalithic site, one that includes the most beautiful *taula* of all, is reached via the minor road from Alaior to Cala N'Porter. Excavations began in 1973 ㉒ ▶ on **Torralba d'en Salort**

The *taula* at Torralba d'en Salort

(June–Sept daily 10am–8pm, Oct–May Mon–Sat 10am–1pm, 3–6pm; charge), but there are still more discoveries to be made. A small bronze statue of a calf was found here (now in the Museu de Menorca), indicating that the bull was worshipped in Menorca as it was in the rest of the Mediterranean.

Cala N'Porter and Cales Coves

Cala N'Porter does not have a great deal of character. The sandy beach is pleasant enough, surrounded by high cliffs, with tall grasses growing where the deep gorge meets the sea, and the waves can be good for surfing, but to reach the sprawling development above you have to climb up a long flight of steps cut into the limestone, or go some distance up a hill. This means that the road train has to work overtime, ferrying people back and forth to their hotels.

   The most popular attraction here is the **Cova d'en Xoroi** (www.covadenxoroi.com; daily 11am–9.30pm; charge), a large cave set in the sheer cliff face some 25m (80ft) above the sea and sky. Although you can't explore the cave itself and the fee is a little steep, the views and the little café terrace are glorious. At night the cave is transformed into a disco, which opens at 11pm and keeps going (loudly) until the early hours.

Just for once, you don't have to go back to the main road. Instead, head towards **Sant Climent** (best known for its jazz club), where there is a substantial English expatriate population. You could make a detour to the development of Son Vitamina, from where you can walk to the impressive **Cales Coves**. **24**

> ### Local legend
>
> According to legend a Moor named Xoroi took refuge in the Cova d'en Xoroi after the reconquest. He eventually abducted a local farmer's daughter and fathered three sons by her. When his hiding place was discovered, Xoroi jumped into the sea and the girl and her children lived (we are told) happily ever after.

Cales Coves was a necropolis but has since had various uses

This is the most important *talayotic* necropolis on the island and one that was still used, for ritual rather than burial purposes, by the Romans. They are put to good use today, as well, by young backpackers who sleep rough in them during the summer, despite occasional attempts by the authorities to keep them away.

Binibeca Vell and its Neighbours

From Sant Climent, take the excellent new road in the direction of Binidalí, parallel with the airport runway. It heralds the beginning of 'the Binis'– the rash of *urbanizaciones* with the Bini prefix (an Arabic legacy) that cover this part of the coast, linked by roads that often lead, frustratingly, to dead ends. There are some nice beaches here, usually accessible only on foot, but the developments are all pretty soulless and similar, until you get to **Binibeca Vell** (also spelled Binibequer Vell).

Architect-designed Binibeca Vell

The houses in this architect-designed 'fishermen's village' – Poblat de Pescadors – washed in brilliant white, look as if they are made of icing sugar. Stairs, chimneys and balconies are all totally harmonious. Narrow, winding alleys emerge into interior courtyards, finished with natural stone and decorated with ceramic tiles; there are palms and orange trees at every corner, and bougainvillaea tumbles over garden walls. Bars and restaurants, a market place, a church and quay have also been constructed as integral parts of the settlement. The vast majority of the apartments and villas are either holiday accommodation or summer homes for people from mainland Spain.

The overall effect is beautiful, but strangely unreal and the hordes of visitors dropped off by tour coaches during the summer months for a quick tour of the village only add to the impression that this is part of a film set. Those old enough to remember the cult 1960s UK television series *The Prisoner* may expect a large balloon to follow them around, blocking their escape from the village.

Sant Lluís and Cala d'Alcaufar

26 Now head about 6km (4 miles) inland to **Sant Lluís**, a friendly town built on a grid pattern by the French during their brief period of occupancy (1756–63). There is a car park by the ornate, dove-capped roundabout as you enter town (and an excellent restaurant opposite, *see page 112*).

Halfway up the main road, the neoclassical parish church stands on one side of the road, while the Ajuntament (town hall) is in a small square on the other.

Situated at the far end of town is the **Molí de Dalt** (May–Oct Mon–Sat 10am–2pm, 5–8pm, usually Sun 11am–1pm, Nov–Apr Mon–Sat 10am–1pm; charge), a lovingly restored windmill that houses a small ethnological museum with a collection of traditional farm tools and milling equipment.

If you have some time to spare on your way back to Maó you could stop off at one final, and very impressive, megalithic site, **Trepucó** (Tue–Fri 9.30am–6pm, Sat–Sun 9.30am–1.30pm; charge), just off the main road. If you prefer a last drink by the sea, there is a string of beach-side developments around the southeastern tip of the island. **Cala d'Alcaufar** is perhaps the nicest, as it has retained some of the atmosphere of the fishing village it always was, long before the tourists arrived. The waterfront is lined with low white buildings and boathouses with brightly painted doors, and fishermen go about their business while visitors sip drinks at café tables, or soak up the sun. From here, or from Sant Lluís, it is just a few kilometres back to the centre of Maó, or to the airport, and your journey's end.

The Molí de Dalt houses a welcoming little museum

WHAT TO DO

OUTDOOR ACTIVITIES

Most outdoor activities in Menorca are those you do on, in or under the water, including diving, sailing, windsurfing, water-skiing, fishing and, of course, swimming. However, the island is also a great place for walking and bird watching, and thousands of visitors come here for those reasons, especially in the spring and autumn, when the mild weather makes walking a pleasure, and numerous species of migrating birds delight birdwatchers. Cycling is a good way of seeing parts of the island that are not readily accessible by road, and much of the terrain is relatively flat and undemanding. And as a consequence of the islanders' love of horses, Menorca is also a good place for riding.

Windsurfing and Sailing

The winds and waves of Menorca are ideal for windsurfing and sailing, and there are numerous places where you can take lessons, rent equipment or just spend your whole day enjoying the water. On the northeast coast, Fornells is the main centre of activity. **Windsurf Fornells** (tel: 971 188 150, www.windfornells.com) offers windsurfing, sailing and water-skiing. The safe, shallow waters here make it a particularly good place for beginners. To the west, **Surf & Sail** in Son Xoriguer (tel: 971 387 105 or mobile 629 749 944, www.surfsailmenorca.com) organises all kinds of activities for all abilities. And in the southeast corner, **Go! Nautic** (tel: 639 631 250 (mobile), www.gonautic.com), offers daily and weekly yacht charters, plus one-day sailing excursions.

Menorca is an ideal place for watersports pros and beginners

Diving

Diving in Menorca's sparkling waters can be an unforgettable experience, and there are many outfits to help you make the most of it. All the organisations mentioned below have instructors trained through PADI (Professional Association of Diving Instructors); check www.padi.com for details.

SUBmorena Divers (Passeig de la Riu, Loc. 7, Cala Galdana, tel: 609 303 760 (mobile), www.dive-centers.net) organises daily diving trips and courses. **Diving Center Fornells** (Passeig Marítim 44B, tel: 971 376 431, www.diving fornells.com) offers diving trips in the protected Northern Reserve, as well as courses and equipment hire, and also has kayaks for hire. **S'Algar Diving** (tel: 971 150 601, www.salgardiving.com) in the southeast takes you to some of the most beautiful diving spots on the island. **Diving Centre Poseidon** (Cala Santandria, tel: 971 382 644, www.bahia-

Snorkelling in Menorca's crystal-clear waters

poseidon.de) is popular, too. There are also daily snorkelling courses for children and beginners and all the necessary equipment is for hire. In the north of the island, **Ulmo Diving Centre Addaia** (tel: 971 359 005) runs trips for qualified divers and courses for beginners, hires equipment and can also organise diving holiday packages. **Seven Fathoms Dive** in Los Delfines, near Ciutadella (tel: 971 388 763, www.sevenfathoms.com) is another popular organisation.

Boat Trips and Boat Hire

The glass-bottomed **Yellow Catamarans** (tel: 639 676 351, www.yellowcatamarans.com) run one-hour trips around Maó's harbour up to eight times a day from their base in Port de Maó. From Ciutadella, the *Fiesta* (tel: 670 214 322) makes day trips to the southern beaches with a stop for a paella and sangria lunch and a swim. In the southwest corner, **Amigos** (tel: 609 961 846) run glass-bottomed boat trips from Cala en Bosc to Cala Trebaluger and Binigaus. There are half-day trips and 'sunset parties' (weather conditions permitting), and you can snorkel from the boat if you bring your own gear. From Es Grau, in the Parc Natural S'Albufera, trips in glass-bottomed boats can be taken out to little Illa d'en Colom and around the estuary (boatmen wait at the harbour; there is no need to book).

Sailing and motor boats can be hired from **Nautic Fun** (Moll de Levant 57, Maó, tel: 971 364 250, www.nauticfun menorca.com). They also run sailing courses and organise fishing charters. Motor boats are also for hire from **Menorca boats** (Carrer Marina 78, Moll Comercial, Ciutadella; tel: 971 484 281, www.menorcaboats.com).

Kayaking

Kayaking is becoming increasingly popular. **Dia Complert Esport d'Aventura** (Passeig Marítim 41, Fornells; tel: 609

670 996, www.diacomplert.com) is a competent organisation that organises kayaking trips in the north of the island.

Hiking

Whether you prefer coastal paths, undulating hills, limestone gorges or tranquil wetlands, hiking – *senderismo* in Spanish – is a delight, especially in spring and autumn. In the southeast, parts of the Camí de Cavalls, the old bridle path that used to run all round the island, can be walked, but much of it is inaccessible. Most hikes are fairly gentle and can be done by any reasonably fit person.

Dia Complert Esport d'Aventura in Fornells *(see page 85 for details)* arranges hiking and biking routes all over the island, including birdwatching excursions. On the south coast, hiking in the Barranc d'Algendar can be organised in Cala Santa Galdana through the **Hotel Cala Galdana** (tel: 971 154 500). For all kinds of outdoor activities, **Menorcaactiva** (tel: 971 352 464 (Maó), or 971 381 550 (Ciutadella), www.menorcaactiva.com), is an outfit worth contacting.

Pony trekking

Riding

Menorca is a great place for horses, and riding – either by the hour or on day-long treks – can be organised at a number of stables, including the **Club Hipic Es Boeret** (tel: 971 151 049) at S'Algar. From the stables at **Son Olivar Nou** (Carretera Ciutadella–Cala en Bosc Km 8, tel: 971 387 108, mobile: 679 980 872), you can ride along Son Saura beach. **Menorca a Cavall**, at Finca Santa Rita (Carretera Maó–Ciutadella Km 24, tel: 971 374 637), organises treks through woodland and along the Cami de Cavalls, the 'horse path' around the island. **Hort de Llucaitx Park** (Carretera Maó–Fornells Km 17, tel: 971 188 607, mobile: 629 392 894), hires horses and ponies, suitable for both adults and children. A Jersey-based firm, **The Riding Company**, organises five-day and week-long riding holidays with accommodation (tel: 01534 745 795, www.theridingcompany.com).

Cycling

Cyclists can take to the inland hills or deep *barrancos* (gorges) on mountain bikes, or simply enjoy coastal paths and wetland trails on conventional cycles. Many resort hotels rent bikes of various kinds. Mountain bikes can be hired in Cala Santa Galdana through the **Rtm Audax Hotel** (tel: 902 356 935, www.artiemhotels.com) who arrange a number of outdoor and sporting activities. Or you could go to **Bike Menorca** (in Maó: Avinguda Francesc Femenies 44, tel: 971 353 798, in Ciutadella: Plaça Menorca s/n, tel: 971 487 827; www.bikemenorca.com). **Dia Complert Esport d'Aventura** in Fornells *(see page 85)* can also organise cycling routes.

Birdwatching

Menorca is a fantastic place for birdwatching, especially in spring and autumn when numerous migrant species break their journeys here. The best sites are the protected wetlands of the **Parc Natural S'Albufera des Grau** (tel: 971 356 303, www.parquesnatrales.consumer.es/documentos/baleares), where cormorants and spoonbills are among the migrants, and booted eagles can be seen in winter, and the **Barranc d'Algendar** in the south (near Cala Santa Galdana), where kestrels and kites are commonly seen wheeling overhead.

Golf

Menorca has one 18-hole, par 72 course, **Golf Son Parc** (tel: 971 188 875, www.golfsonparc.com), on the northeast coast, adjacent to the urbanisation of the same name. They organise golfing holidays, including 'Learn Golf in a Week' packages.

Parc Natural de S'Albufera

CHILDREN'S MENORCA

Menorca is a good place to take small children, as the safe, shallow waters and clean sands keep them happy for hours, and the islanders are welcoming and very child-friendly. The following is a selection of things to do when the beach begins to pall. Boat trips are always popular, and while an hour-long trip around Maó's harbour may not inspire children with an interest in

A giant tap in the children's playground at Santa Galdana

naval history, there's much to see, from ruined castles to giant cruise ships, and the sea bed to examine from an observation gallery when you reach the mouth of the harbour. **Yellow Catamarans** (tel: 639 676 351) is the best known of several companies that run regular one-hour trips *(see page 85)*.

Water parks are always popular in hot weather, and **Aqua Park** in Urbanización Los Delfines (Cala en Blanes; tel: 971 388 705; May–Aug daily 10.30am–6pm, Sept–Oct Tue, Thur, Sun 10.30am–6pm) has, as it claims, something for all the family, with hidro-tubes, a giant toboggan, a children's water chute and bouncy castles, as well as a jacuzzi for parents. **Aquarock** (Cala en Bosc, tel: 971 387 822/971 387 217; May–Oct daily 10.30am– 6pm) has all the usual water park diversions, while **Club San Jaime** in Sant Jaume Mediterrani, near Son Bou (tel: 971 372 787; May–Oct daily 10am–7pm) has a large water chute and a wooden maze, among numerous other attractions.

Leaving the water behind, **Hort de Llucaitx Park** (Carretera Maó–Fornells Km 17, Son Parc; tel: 971 188 607/629 392 894; May–Oct daily 10am–8pm, Nov–Apr Sat–Sun only) is fun, with pony trekking, mini-golf and playgrounds as well as adult activities. At **Son Olivar Nou** *(see page 86)* there are donkeys, ponies, goats, pigs and chickens, as well as pony rides, to keep smaller children amused.

On the Carretera Ferreries–Cala Santa Galdana are two places that put on regular spectacular equestrian shows, which are suitable for children and adults (although seem to be particularly popular with young girls), during the summer months. **Son Martorellet** (mobile: 639 156 851, www.sonmartorellet.com) and the **Club Escola Menorquina** (tel: 971 155 059) offer similar shows, although the former is larger, more elaborate and rather more expensive. It is also possible to visit the stables and watch the horses being put through their paces (call the above numbers for details of times and prices).

Both Aquapark and Aquarock have go-kart tracks, and **Karting Menorca** (tel: 971 380 424; daily 10am–8pm), located in the big El Castillo shopping and leisure complex on the Carretera Maó–Ciutadella (Me-1), about 12km (7½ miles) east of Ciutadella, is hard to miss.

SHOPPING

Leather

The best things to buy in Menorca are leather goods – the island is justly famous for its long-established leather industry. Shoes, bags and belts are the things to go for, but coats and jackets are good value, too. Ciutadella, Ferreries and Alaior are the main centres of production. Especially interesting are *abarcas*, the flat, slipper-like sandals that have been worn by peasants for centuries. They have grown less

Crafting *abarcas*

simple in recent years, and a whole range of subtle and striking colours is now available, some with delicate hand-painted patterns. Shop around, because prices vary.

At Maó's **S'Abarca** (Moll de Levant 21), the sandals are made on the premises; they are not necessarily cheaper or better than those you buy elsewhere but you can choose the colour and design. **Calçats Truyol** is a small chain that stocks some lovely designs, with branches in Maó (Carrer d'en Deià 9) and Ferreries (Carrer Pau Pons 12). In Ciutadella, **TR3S** (Carrer Quadrado 18, Ses Voltes) has a good selection.

For classy bags and belts, visit Ciutadella's **Iñaki Sampedro** (Carrer Seminari 36) or Maó's **Marisa** (Carrer Hannover 7, Costa de Sa Plaça). Internationally known **Pons Quintana** sells lovely shoes in its shops in Maó (at S'Arravaleta 21), in Ciutadella (at Contramurada 95), and in Alaior at Sant Antoni 120. **Jaime Mascaro** is the other well-known shoe company on the island, and has a shop in Maó at Carrer Ses

Traditional *abarcas*

Moreres 29. The goods you find in the Mascaro factory outlet on the Poligono Industrial, on the Me-1 near Ferreries, are not always as good as those you will find in smaller shops. This is true of all the other large-scale emporiums strung along the Me-1. Some provide restaurants and children's playgrounds to attract customers, but they are not the best places to shop.

You will see the sign **Pou Nou** in shops all over the island. This is a Menorcan designer T-shirt company, but they also make other casual wear, and their quality, colours and designs are good. **S'Ecològica de Menorca** use only chlorine-free, water-based paints on their attractive T-shirts and casuals, with designs by Menorcan artist Jaume Bagur. You will find them in numerous outlets all over the island.

Food and Drink

The food most worth taking home is cheese, **Queso de Mahón** *(see page 103)*. It is actually made in Alaior, and you can buy it at the factory outlets there: **La Payesa**, Carrer des Banyer 64 and **Coingo**, Carrer Es Mercadel 8. If you don't get to Alaior, don't worry – it is sold all over the island, and even at the airport, packed in distinctive boxes. At **Hort de Sant Patrici** (Camí de Sant Patrici, Ferreries; tel: 971 373 702), you can watch the cheese being made and taste it before buying. The shop keeps normal hours, but to see the production process go on Mon–Wed, Fri–Sat 9–11am.

Ensaimadas, the sugar-dusted pastries that are an island speciality, can be bought in *confiterías* (pastry shops) and speciality stores everywhere, and come in all sizes, the larger ones often packed in special boxes. There's a good selection in the old-fashioned **Confitería Miguel Bagur** (Ses Voltes 8, Ciutadella) and in **El Turronero** (Carrer Nou 22, Maó), a shop established in 1894 that also sells Xoriguer gin, Queso de Mahón, local figs and *turrón*, an almond-based delicacy, that can be soft like fudge, or hard, rather like nougat.

Colmado La Palma (Carrer Hannover, Costa Sa Plaça 15), has a good selection of cured Mahón cheese and almond biscuits. In Ciutadella, **Bon Gust** (Camí de Maó 20), sells a range of local products, including cheese bottled in oil.

Ensaimadas for breakfast – if you're not on a diet

Xoriguer gin, packaged in bottles with handles on the neck, can be sampled and purchased at the Xoriguer distillery outlet, Moll de Ponent 93, Maó, and in their shop at Plaça del Carme 16, but it's available everywhere, as is *pomada*, a gin-and-lemonade drink, and a variety of colourful herbal liqueurs. Menorca is not known for its wines, but **Bodegas Binifadet** is producing some excellent vintages. Their chardonnay has

Gin distillery

received particular praise. Buy in specialist food shops or visit the winery outside San Lluis (tel: 971 150 715) for tours and tastings.

Ceramics

Two of the best places on the island to buy **pottery** are **Hermanos Lora Buzón** (Moll de Ponent 10) and **S'Alambic** (Moll de Ponent 35) in Maó. Both shops have interesting and unusual handmade items, and will be pleased to manufacture to order and ship your goods home, although there are quite a lot of run-of-the-mill souvenirs on sale in both places as well.

Markets

Morning markets are held in all towns on Menorca, both outdoors or in covered market halls. They usually sell clothes, household items and sometimes craftwork as well as food. The biggest and most colourful food markets are held from Monday to Saturday in the **Claustre del Carme** in Maó and the **Plaça de la Libertat** in Ciutadella. Ferreries holds a renowned farmers' market on Saturday morning, when local produce and craftwork are for sale. Alaior's market is on Monday and Thursday, Es Castell's on Monday and Wednesday, Es Migjorn Gran's on Wednesday, Es Mercadel's on Sunday and Fornells' on Thursday.

NIGHTLIFE AND ENTERTAINMENT

Menorca is not really the place to go for nightlife. There are clubs and discos in the bigger resorts but the island does not really attract the clubbing crowd. **Cova d'en Xoroi** disco (tel: 971 137 236), is the most unusual, dramatically set in the cliff in Cala N'Porter *(see page 78)*.

A few places worth trying in Maó are the music bar **Mambo** (Moll de Llevant 209), which has loud music inside and a pleasant terrace outside, **Akelaare** (Moll de Ponent 41), a vaulted cocktail bar that plays jazz, blues and modern music, and trendy **Café Mo Blues** (Carrer Santiago Ramón i Cajal 3), which also plays jazz and blues. In Ciutadella, try **Sa Clau Jazz Club** in the Marina for jazz, cocktails and single-malt whiskies. **Jazzbah** (Pla de Sant Joan 4, by the port) holds popular live sessions, starting at 8pm. Also in the port is **Asere**, a lively salsa club with music every evening during the summer months. **Casino Sant Climent** (Carrer Sant Jaume 4) in Sant Climent is something of an institution, and hosts good live jazz on Tuesday and Thursday.

The only casino is **Casino Marítim** (Moll de Levant 287, Maó; tel: 971 364 962; restaurant 9pm–2am, casino 9pm–5am). You should dress smartly and take your passport or driving licence for identification purposes.

Theatrical performances, are in Spanish or Catalan, of course, but the **Teatre Principal** (tel: 971 355 776) stages interesting musical events, where language is not a problem.

For cool Menorcan jazz

FESTIVALS

Many of the festivals in Menorca revolve around the *jaleo*, a dance performed by horses, orchestrated by skilled riders – *caixers*. The two major events are the Festes de Sant Joan, in Ciutadella, and the Festes de la Vierge de Gràcia, in Maó. Sant Joan is celebrated on 23–24 June, and on the previous Sunday, the 'Día des Be', a man representing John the Baptist, dressed in sheepskins, walks barefoot through the old town of Ciutadella, accompanied by the *caixers* (also on foot at this stage), inviting everyone to the fiesta. On the 23rd the celebrations start with the *primer toc*, the first notes of a flute called a *flabiol*. Then Ciutadella goes wild, with crowds of people thronging into the Plaça d'es Born and neighbouring streets to witness horseback processions and jousting tournaments. The horsemen, dressed in black and white and decorated with ribbons, embroidery and carnations, ride among the crowds, prancing and circling on their horses' hind legs. The longer a horse manages to stay on two legs, the greater the appreciation of the crowd, which surges forward, oblivious of flailing hooves, trying to get as close as possible to the action.

Horsemanship at Maó's
Festa de Gràcia

The festival honouring the Vierge de Gràcia in Maó on 7–9 September, is equally raucous, with colourful processions and music, and similar stunning displays of horsemanship and daring in the flag-bedecked streets. Both events are crowned by magnificent firework displays on the final evening.

Calendar of Events

17 January: Fests d'es Tres Tocs – Festival of the Three Blows – is held in Ciutadella to commemorate the reconquest of Menorca in 1287.

Mid- to late February: Carnival (Carnaval) is celebrated in many towns and villages, with fancy dress parades and general revelry. The date varies as it is a pre-Lent festival.

Late March–April: Semana Santa (Holy Week) is celebrated throughout the island with solemn processions. Festivities in Maó and Ciutadella are the most impressive.

23–24 June: Festes de Sant Joan in Ciutadella. Two days of spectacular equestrian displays *(see page 59)*, music and general fun, crowned by a magnificent fireworks display.

15–16 July: Día del Virgen de Carmen. The patron saint of fishermen and sailors is celebrated in many ports with processions of decorated boats on the water. Maó, Ciutadella and Fornells are the principal venues.

18–21 July: Sant Martí is celebrated in Es Mercadal with secular and religious events.

25–28 July: Festa de Sant Antoní in Fornells, in honour of the patron saint of the village. The processions are crowned by a magnificent *jaleo* (horses' dance) at the harbour.

July–September: Classical-music festivals are held on various dates throughout these summer months in Maó and Ciutadella, and in August in Fornells. Contact the relevant tourist offices for details.

2–4 August: Es Migjorn Gran celebrates its patron saint, Sant Cristòfal.

8–10 August: Sant Llorenç is celebrated in Alaior, with a pilgrimage made to Binixems.

24–25 August: Sant Bartomeu is celebrated in Ferreries, with a *jaleo* (see above).

7–9 September: Festes de la Vierge de Gràcia. The Virgin of Monte Toro is honoured with a huge celebration in Maó.

12–14 September: Sant Nicolau is celebrated in Es Mercadal and El Toro with processions, a *jaleo*, music and folk dancing, as well as a religious ceremony at the sanctuary on top of Monte El Toro.

EATING OUT

Those who find food one of the greatest pleasures of foreign travel will not be disappointed in Menorca. Whether you are eating out in restaurants, or buying food in local markets to cook in the kitchen of your self-catering apartment or take on picnics, you'll find the choice wide and interesting. You won't find the best of it in the resort restaurants catering mainly to northern European tourists, which tend to fall back on 'international cuisine', but steer clear of these and you will find plenty of places serving good, authentic food (see pages 107–13 for some recommendations). You may also find, when wandering past a row of harbour-side restaurants, that their menus look pretty much the same, and there is little – including the price – to tell you which is superior to its neighbour. The clientele is a fairly reliable guide: too few customers is a bad sign, of course, but a very full restaurant may be one that caters largely to tour groups, and the food may therefore be rather bland. The number of Spanish- or Catalan-speakers eating in an establishment usually indicates that the food and service are good and that you will get value for money.

Richelieu's sauce

Salsa mahonesa – mayonnaise – originated on the island in the 18th century. The story goes that a local chef made it for the Duke of Richelieu, leader of the French forces that drove the British (temporarily) from the island in 1756, and he took the recipe back to Paris with him. In another version, the cook was Richelieu's mistress, and he named it after her – la mahonesa.

Cuina Menorquina

It is in restaurants advertising cuina menorquina that you will find the true island food. Tumbet is a dish of

Fornells' fish restaurants are well regarded

peppers, aubergines, tomatoes and potatoes, coated in beaten egg and baked in the oven. This often features as a first course, but can be very filling, so should be followed by something light. *Trempó* is also served as a first course: described as a salad it can be more like a rather solid *gazpacho*, made of finely chopped tomatoes, peppers, onions, capers and lots of garlic in oil and vinegar – good, as long as you really like garlic. Don't get confused with *coca de trempó*, which is a kind of pizza with tomatoes, green peppers and onions. *Conejo con higos* (rabbit with dried figs), *cordero con cebollas y alcaparras* (lamb with onions and capers) and *cabrito al horno* (roast kid) are substantial and delicious oven-baked dishes. *Escaldums*, a stew of chicken, meat balls, potatoes and vegetables, is tasty and very filling. *Berenjenos relleños* (stuffed aubergines) are also very popular. Queso de Mahón *(see page 103)* is often used in salads or melted on baked vegetables. *Espinacas à la catalana –*

spinach cooked with garlic, anchovies, raisins and pine nuts – is a first course found on many menus.

Soups are popular, too, including *escudella*, a soup of mixed vegetables, and *sopas mallorquinas* (a Mallorcan dish always referred to in this plural form). The latter is a combination of vegetables, olives, garlic and sometimes pork, more like a stew than a soup, and a substantial first course.

Fish Dishes

In most island restaurants, but especially those in Maó, Ciutadella and Fornells you will find a wide range of fresh fish *(pescado)* on offer, in many guises. *Lubina* (sea bass), *dorado* (gilthead bream), *besugo* (sea bream) are cooked either on a grill *(a la plancha)* or in the oven *(al horno)*. They are often prepared in an outer casing of sea salt before being baked; you would imagine this would make the fish very

One of the lobster dishes typical of Menorca

salty but it doesn't, and the taste is delicious. *Sardinas a la plancha* (grilled sardines) are found on many menus. A *parillada de pescado* is a mixture of grilled fish. *Suquet* is a rich fish stew, and *bacalao* is cod, salted and dried. It is not to everyone's taste, but when well prepared it can be good, especially in *esqueixada*, a salad of tomatoes, onions and shredded salt cod.

Mussels straight from the sea are delicious

Calamares (squid), *sepia* (cuttlefish) and *pulpo* (octopus), cooked in a variety of ways, are widely available. *Calamares en su tinta* is squid cooked in its own ink; *a la romana* means it is cut into rings and fried in batter.

Caldereta de llagosta is the star among Menorcan fish dishes. It is the speciality of the fish restaurants of Fornells, but also features on menus in the port of Maó and Ciutadella. A thick stew is prepared using lobster, tomatoes, onions, green pepper, garlic, parsley, egg yolk and brandy, then poured on to slices of bread and served. Cooks all have their own recipes, so the dish is never quite the same from place to place. It is rich and delicious and the only disadvantage is the price – around €50–55 a person, and it is always made for two.

There are two cheaper variations, however: *caldereta de mariscos*, a thick shellfish soup, and *caldereta de pescado*, which contains several different kinds of fish.

Puddings and Pastries
Home-made *crème caramel*, *crema Catalana*, or it's mass-produced cousin, known as a *flan*, is as ubiquitous on the

The island's famous cheese

Balearics as the mainland, but there are also some wonderful sweet pastries and the almond-and-honey desserts that are a delicious legacy of the Moorish occupation. *Ensaimadas* are the pastries you are most likely to see on sale, a light and airy concoction that's rolled up like a turban, dusted with sugar, and often eaten for breakfast. Large, family-sized versions are also sold, sometimes in plywood boxes, and these make attractive, typically Menorcan gifts to take home if you have room in your luggage. Vegetarians should be aware that lard *(saim)* is an essential Menorcan ingredient and a key element in the *ensaimada*. *Crespells*, a kind of shortbread biscuit, and *amargos* almond-flavoured biscuits are also popular.

Shopping for Food

If you are on a self-catering holiday and shopping for food in the markets, you will be able to choose from a wide variety of vegetables, depending on the season. Glossy aubergines, large, misshapen but delicious tomatoes and courgettes, and wonderfully fresh spinach will help you make authentic Mediterranean dishes to accompany the fresh fish that glistens on beds of ice, or meat, which is cut to order by the butcher. If you are making up a picnic, local cheese, chorizo, tomatoes and seasonal fruit, together with a loaf of fresh bread, may be all you need.

Eating Habits

As in the rest of Spain, people in Menorca tend to eat late: lunch is generally between 1.30 and 3.30pm, and 10pm is a popular time for dinner. However, restaurateurs, well aware that Northern European visitors prefer to eat earlier, have adapted their timetables accordingly, and some serve food throughout the day. Remember not to write off a restaurant that looks alarmingly empty at 8.30pm because it may be buzzing with local people and visitors two hours later. Be aware that many restaurants close for several months in winter and many close one day a week, usually Monday or Tuesday.

Many places offer a *menú del día*, a daily set menu that is a real bargain; it is always available at lunchtime and sometimes in the evening too. For a fixed price (around €15), you will get three courses – a starter, which is often soup or salad, a main fish or meat dish and a dessert, generally ice cream, a piece of fruit or a *flan* (caramel custard),

Queso de Mahón

The British introduced the dairy industry to Menorca in the 18th century, and it flourished. Not only will you see lots of cows as you travel around the island, but also many huge advertisements for cheese – Queso de Mahón. Despite the name, most of it is made in Alaior and despite mechanisation, most is still made in the traditional manner. It is produced from cow's milk with just a little ewe's milk added, which gives it a distinctive flavour. The whey is separated from the set milk and the cheese is soaked for a day in salt water and left for a month on a rack, where it is turned regularly. The varieties depend on how long they have aged, so you get *tierno* (young), *semi-curado* (semi-mature), *curado* (mature) and *añejo* (very mature indeed), with a texture similar to parmesan. You can buy it in any grocer's or gift shop, or even at the airport, but for details of the factory outlets in Alaior, see page 51.

plus a glass of wine, beer or bottled water and bread.

Reservations are recommended only at more expensive restaurants, or at Sunday lunchtime in popular spots. Prices sometimes include service – look for *servicio incluido* on the bill – but if not it is customary to leave a 10 percent tip.

Tapas

Tapas, the popular Spanish snacks, have not caught on in Menorca as they have in other parts of Spain. You do find some tapas bars, though – more in Ciutadella than in Maó. *Calamares* (squid), *albóndigas* (meat balls), spicy *chorizo*, and *boquerones* (marinated anchovy fillets), are among the most ubiquitous, often accompanied by *pa amb tomàquet*, bread rubbed with oil, garlic and tomato.

Drinks

Wine is usually drunk with meals, much of it imported from the Spanish mainland; Riojas and varieties from the Catalan Penedès region feature prominently. There is virtually no wine made commercially on Menorca; you will

Xoriguer gin – made in Maó, drunk all over the island

sometimes, but not often, see Mallorcan wines, most of which come from the region around Binissalem. Spanish beer is also popular, especially with young people. Fresh orange juice *(zumo de naranja)* is refreshing, and those who like the flavour of almonds should try *horchata de chufa*, a milky drink made from ground almonds that is served ice cold in summer.

Locally made Xoriguer gin is sold everywhere, but waiters will often ask visitors if they would prefer one of the more expensive internationally known brands. Ask for *nacional* if you want to try the island gin. You will also see *pomada*, which is gin mixed with lemonade. There are lots of herbal liqueurs – *hierbas* – as well, which sometimes come in frighteningly vivid colours.

Coffee is drunk at breakfast and throughout the day. *Café con leche* is a large one with lots of hot milk; with a *cortado*, usually served in a glass, you get the same amount of coffee with just a

A waterfront bar in Maó

splash of milk. A *café solo* is a small, strong black coffee, and with an *americano* you get added hot water.

Bars and Cafés

In towns, some bars and cafés open at first light to cater for early-morning workers, and the majority are open by 8.30am for breakfast. One of the great pleasures of the Mediterranean is sitting in a square in the morning with a coffee and croissant and watching a town come to life. In resorts, however, where most tourists breakfast in their hotels, you may have more difficulty finding somewhere for an early coffee. At many open-air cafés you can get a selection of sandwiches – *bocadillos* in Spanish, *entrepans* in Catalan – at most hours.

TO HELP YOU ORDER

Could we have a table, please?	**¿Nos puede dar una mesa, por favor?**
Do you have a set menu?	**¿Tiene un menú del día?**
I'd like…	**Quisiera…**
The bill, please	**La cuenta, por favor**

MENU READER

agua	water	**al punto**	medium
vino	wine	**buen hecho**	well done
leche	milk	**asado**	roast
cerveza	beer	**a la plancha**	grilled
pan	bread	**al ajillo**	in garlic
ensalada	salad	**picante**	spicy
tortilla	omelette	**salsa**	sauce
pescado	fish	**cocido**	stew
mariscos	shellfish	**jamón serrano**	cured ham
langosta	lobster		
calamares	squid	**chorizo**	spicy sausage
mejillones	mussels		
anchoas	anchovies	**bocadillo**	sandwich
atún	tuna	**arroz**	rice
bacalao	dried cod	**verduras**	vegetables
cangrejo	crab	**champiñones**	mushrooms
pulpo	octopus	**habas**	broad beans
trucha	trout	**espinacas**	spinach
carne	meat	**cebollas**	onions
cerdo/lomo	pork	**lentejas**	lentils
ternera	veal	**queso**	cheese
cordero	lamb	**postre**	dessert
buey/res	beef	**helado**	ice cream
pollo	chicken	**azúcar**	sugar
conejo	rabbit	**flan**	caramel custard
poco hecho	rare		

PLACES TO EAT

We have used the following symbols to give an idea of the price for a three-course meal for one, including wine, cover and service:

€ below 30 euros
€€ 30–45 euros
€€€ 45–75 euros

MAÓ AND ES CASTELL

Andaira €€–€€€ *Carrer des Forn 61, tel: 971 366 817.* Proving that all the best restaurants don't have to be by the harbour (although most are), the Andaira serves interesting Mediterranean dishes in a discreet green-shuttered town house with a courtyard, close to the Plaça d'Esplanada. Usually open for dinner only, but check, as hours vary throughout the year.

Can Chimichurri €€ *Carrer Gran 67, Es Castells, tel: 971 356 983.* Housed in a typical 19th-century building, this Argentinian restaurant serves lots of barbecued meat accompanied by wines from Argentina and Chile. Seafood and vegetables are also available, prepared with care. Fri and Sat only in winter.

Gregal €€–€€€ *Moll de Llevant 306, tel: 971 366 606.* Located at the Cala Figuera end of the harbour, this restaurant produces a range of imaginative fish dishes, and is a great local favourite. It has been here for more than 25 years. Try the delicious *merluza* (hake), served on a bed of black rice, or the fried sea anemones.

Il Porto €–€€ *Moll de Llevant 225, tel: 971 354 426.* Come here for a relaxed atmosphere, good Italian food and an excellent wine list. The *parillada de verduras* (mixed grilled vegetables) are especially good, as is the *lubina* (sea bass).

Irene €€ *Carrer Sa Font 1, Cales Fonts, Es Castell, tel: 971 354 788.* Set on the road above the harbour with an outside terrace, this restaurant does well-cooked traditional Spanish dishes and tapas, and offers a reasonably priced set menu in the evenings.

L'Arpó €€ *Moll de Llevant 124, tel: 971 369 844.* A pleasant bistro, specialising in fish. *Cap Roig* (scorpion fish) is a popular choice. Great views over the harbour.

La Minerva €€€ *Moll de Llevant 87, tel: 971 351 995.* The main restaurant is set in an old flour mill, but you can also eat on the floating jetty. Paella is a speciality. Elegant and expensive, although the tasting menu offers excellent value.

Meson del Port €€ *Moll de Ponent 66, tel: 971 352 903/340 175.* Good, substantial Basque cooking in a traditional-style restaurant near the ferry terminal and the Xoriguer gin factory. Lots of interesting starters, including stuffed artichokes *(alcachofas rellenos)* and some delicious cured hams.

Roma €€ *Moll de Llevant 267, tel: 971 353 777.* Excellent pizzas, pasta and other Italian specialities, fair prices and a cheerful atmosphere ensure that Roma is always busy. Serves food all day from 12.30pm to midnight. Closed Tue.

S'Espigó €€€ *Moll de Llevant 295, tel: 971 369 909.* Another reliably good harbour-side restaurant, specialising mostly in fish and seafood. Try the artichokes with prawns or baby peppers stuffed with fish for starters. Closed Sun lunch.

Siroco €–€€ *Moll des Cales Fonts 39, Cales Fonts, Es Castell, tel: 971 367 965.* Reasonable food at reasonable prices, served by friendly staff – a formula that seems to work, judging by the number of regular customers greeted with kisses and handshakes. Paella is popular, and you could make a whole meal of the tapasstyle starters.

Treból €€ *Moll des Cales Fonts 43, Cales Fonts, Es Castell, tel: 971 367 097.* A long-established and popular fish restaurant built into the cliff on the attractive Cales Fonts harbour side. Open daily in summer till 1am.

Varadero €€€ *Moll de Llevant 4, tel: 971 352 074*. Beside the Port Authority building this smart, minimalist restaurant has a menu that includes salmon cooked in *cava*. To enjoy the atmosphere and spend less, have a drink and a snack in the bar.

CIUTADELLA

Café Balear €€ *Pla de Sant Joan 15, Port de Ciutadella, tel: 971 380 005*. An excellent litle restaurant at the east end of the harbour, just past the pedestrian bridge. Some say that the *caldereta de llagosta* (lobster stew) is the best in Menorca, although no one in Fornells would agree. There's a delicious choice of starters, from *gambas a la plancha* (grilled prawns) to *calamares rebozados* (squid in batter).

Ca'n Nito € *Plaça des Born 11, tel: 971 480 768*. An unassuming café on the square, that serves good tapas day and night. The anchovies *(anchoas)* are recommended.

Ca's Quintú (Club Náutic) €€€ *Camí de Baix (under Passeig de Sant Nicolau), tel: 971 382 773*. An elegant restaurant in the yacht club, specialising in fish and seafood. Enjoy an aperitif on the large terrace overlooking the harbour.

Casa Manolo €€–€€€ *Carrer Marina 117, Port de Ciutadella, tel: 971 380 003*. At the far end of the harbour promenade, Manolo's has been established for nearly as long as the port – well, for over four decades anyway. There's a wide choice of freshly caught fish, from clams to *caldereta de llagosta*.

D'es Port €€€ *Carrer Marina 23, Port de Ciutadella, tel: 971 480 022*. Set into the cliff and with tables on the quayside, this smart blue-and-white restaurant serves excellent fish. As well as *caldereta de llagosta* there's *suquet* (fish stew), *paella*, of course, and *esqueixada*, a salad of tomatoes, onions and salt cod. Service is attentive but not overwhelming. Open daily till midnight.

El Bribón €€ *Carrer Marina 115, Port de Ciutadella, tel: 971 385 050*. By the time you reach this end of the marina (it's next door to Manolo's), you may feel as if you have read the same menu too many times over. El Bribón's isn't that different from the rest, but they serve reliably good food at reasonable prices and there's a good set menu for €13.

El Horno €€ *Carrer des Forn 12, tel: 971 380 767*. If you can tear yourself away from sunset over the harbour – which can be difficult on a lovely evening – this small basement restaurant tucked into a narrow street at the back of Plaça d'es Born serves good *comida casera* – traditional local food.

La Guitarra €€ *Carrer dels Dolors 1, tel: 971 381 355*. Another place that makes it worth leaving the harbour for lunch or an evening meal. Close to the Plaça de la Catedral this well-run and long-established cellar restaurant serves authentic *cuina menorquina: conejo con cebollas* (rabbit with onions), *escaldums* (chicken, meatballs and vegetables) and much more.

Pa amb Oli € *Carrer Nou de Juliol 4 (just off Plaça d'es Born), tel: 971 383 619*. *Pa amb oli* means bread and oil in Catalan, and that is exactly what you get: toasted country bread, which you rub with whole cloves of garlic, tomato, and olive oil, and eat with a choice of toppings: ham, sausage, tuna, grilled vegetables, etc. There are other things to eat in this cheerful place, but this is what the majority of people come for.

Racó des Palau €€ *Carrer des Palau 3, tel 971 385 402*. Tucked away in a back street behind the Palau Salort, the Racó has been here for many years, and serves good Spanish and local dishes in a comfortable atmosphere.

THE NORTHEAST

ES GRAU

Tamarindos €–€€ *Pas d'es Tamarells 14, tel: 971 359 420*. The fish dishes in this unpretentious little place are wholesome, simple and taste all the better for being served on a wooden terrace so close to the sea you could almost catch them yourself.

FORNELLS

El Pescador €€ *Plaça s'Algaret 3, tel: 971 376 538.* There is a pleasant terrace on the promenade, ceramic plates with crustacean motifs on the walls, and a wide-ranging fish menu. A *menú del día* is available in the evening as well as at lunch time.

Es Cranc €€ *Carrer Escoles 31, tel: 971 376 442.* Tucked away in the old town, but only a few minutes' walk from the harbour, Es Cranc serves imaginative meat dishes, fresh fish and seafood. Popular with islanders and visitors from Barcelona, so it's best to book at weekends.

Es Cranc Pelut €€€ *Gumersindo Riera 98 (Passeig Marítim), tel: 971 376 743.* Despite the confusingly similar name (Es Cranc means 'The Crab' and this is 'The Hairy Crab') the two restaurants are quite different. On the seafront, this one specialises in *caldereta de llagosta* and other seafood, and its renowned chef, Diego Coll, has produced a book on Menorcan cooking.

Es Pla €€–€€€ *Carrer Gumersindo Riera (Passeig Marítim) s/n, tel: 971 376 655.* A tastefully decorated seafood restaurant right beside the harbour – not separated from it by the road, as the others are. This is where Juan Carlos comes for his *caldereta de llagosta*, when the royal yacht is anchored in the harbour. The paella is excellent, too. Booking essential for Sunday lunch.

Es Port €€ *Carrer Gumersindo Riera 5 (Passeig Marítim), tel: 971 376 403.* Friendly and extremely relaxed, this harbour-side restaurant makes a delicious *caldereta*. The *lubina* (sea bass) and *dorada* (gilthead bream), baked in a crust of salt, are excellent, too, and come at considerably more affordable prices. Also has a good wine list.

Sa Llagosta €€€ *Carrer Gabriel Gelabert 12, tel: 971 376 566.* Very smart, very discreet, this establishment serves such delights as *calamares* with green risotto, and baked fish dishes, including *rodaballo* (turbot) and *pargo* (sea bream), as well as lobster in many guides, including *caldereta de llagosta* (lobster stew).

THE SOUTH

CALA BLANCA

Es Caliu €€ *Carretera Ciutadella–Cala en Bosc, tel: 971 380 165*. Good barbecued meat is the speciality of this big, busy restaurant.

CALA EN BOSC

Café Balear €€ *Carrer Portitxol 16, tel: 971 387 368*. A sister restaurant to the one of the same name in Ciutadella *(see page 109)*, Café Balear does excellent grilled meat, including steaks and brochettes, as well as the fish for which it is renowned.

SANT LLUÍS

La Venta de Paco €€ *Avinguda Sant Pau 158, tel: 971 150 995/971 150 793*. Situated right by the roundabout as you enter town from the south, La Venta serves splendid *cuina menorquina*, with interesting options including grilled suckling pig *(lechona), cordero* (lamb) and *cabrito* (kid).

Pan y Vino €€ *Camí de la Coixa/Carrer Torret, Torret, tel: 610 319 279*. Located in the village of Torret, just to the south of Sant Lluís, this intimate restaurant has a French chef, and serves excellent oven-baked fish and meat and game dishes, such as roast partridge. It is very popular with the local expatriates, so booking is advisable. Tables on an outdoor terrace in summer.

THE CENTRE

ALAIOR

Sa Palmereta €€ *Carrer Sant Pancraç 7, tel: 971 372 971*. A very pretty restaurant that comes well recommended. Meat and fish dishes are served with seasonal vegetables and interesting accompaniments and there is a good wine list, including some Mallorcan wines.

ES MERCADAL

Ca n'Aguedet €€ *Carrer Lepanto 23–30, tel: 971 375 391.* Some of the island's best *cuina menorquina* in a restaurant that has been here since 1936. Rabbit, lamb and suckling pig *(lechona)* among other things are served in a light and airy first-floor dining room reached via a white marble staircase. Surprisingly reasonable prices. Booking advisable at weekends.

Ca n'Olga €€ *Pont Na Macarrana, tel: 971 375 459.* Hidden behind an archway near the river, this place serves good *cuina menorquina* on a large terrace or in a stylishly furnished dining room. *Mariscos* (seafood), *cordoniz* (quail) and *conejo* (rabbit) are all recommended, and *Cap Roig* (scorpion fish) is one of the house specialities. Booking is advisable.

Molí d'es Racó €€ *Carrer Vicario Fuxà 53, tel: 971 375 392.* Set in an old mill with a large terrace, just off the Me-1. The Menorcan cooking is good, but note that the restaurant caters to large coach parties, and service can get a bit rushed at times.

ES MIGJORN GRAN

58, S'Engolidor €€ *Carrer Major 3, tel: 971 370 193.* Islanders and visitors come from far and wide to eat here, and with good reason. In a series of little dining rooms and alcoves or outside on a shady terrace, attentive and friendly waiters serve delicious *cuina menorquina*, including *dorado con alcaparras* (gilthead bream with capers) and *conejo con mostaza* (rabbit with mustard sauce) as well as home-made puddings. From the terrace there are wonderful views over the S'Engolidor *barranco*. Booking is essential. Apr–Oct Tue–Sun; serves dinner only.

FERRERIES

Mesón El Gallo €–€€ *Carretera Cala Santa Galdana Km 1.5, tel: 971 373 039.* A farmhouse restaurant just outside town on the way to Cala Galdana, 'The Cockerel' has been in business for many years. It is renowned for its good-quality grilled meat.

A–Z TRAVEL TIPS

A Summary of Practical Information

A

ACCOMMODATION (See also Camping, and the list of Recommended Hotels on pages 134–41)

Hotel prices are not government controlled, but rates have to be posted at reception desks and in rooms. Off-season, you can get much lower rates but many hotels close from November to Easter. In high season, many resort hotels are block-booked by tour operators.

Accommodation ranges across a broad spectrum, although there are not many *pensions* (guest houses). *Hostales* (modest hotels) are graded from one to three stars while *hoteles* (hotels) are rated from one to five stars. Grades are more a reflection of facilities than quality: some two-star places can be superior to others with four. There is a blurring of categories, however: *pensions* may call themselves *hostales* and vice-versa; some hotels also call themselves *hostales*.

Small hotels in rural settings and refurbished farmhouses and manor houses are called *finca* or *agroturisme* properties. They range from rustic to luxurious; many have pools and tennis courts. Some are listed at www.menorcaturismorural.net.

Package deals are the cheapest way to holiday in Menorca; accommodation is nearly always in the busiest resorts, but can provide an economical base from which to explore the island. Packages offering accommodation in furnished apartments or villas are also popular. They are usually part of a complex with amenities, such as a pool, gardens and sports facilities.

I would like a single/ double room	**Quisiera una habitación sencilla/doble**
with/without bathroom and toilet/shower	**con/sin baño/ducha**
What's the rate per night?	**¿Cuál es el precio por noche?**
Is breakfast included?	**¿Está incluído el desayuno?**

AIRPORT (Aeropuerto)

Maó's compact little airport (MAH) is 5km (3 miles) from the city centre. It is about a 15-minute taxi ride (around €10–12); there is an airport bus service (tel: 902 075 066) to Maó, every 30 minutes in summer, with reduced service in winter. For airport information tel: 902 404 704; airport taxi rank tel: 971 482 222.

B

BICYCLE AND SCOOTER HIRE (Bicicletas de aquiler)

Bikes can be hired in most of the resorts – hotels and tourist offices have leaflets, and you'll be handed flyers in the street. In Maó, contact Bike Menorca (Av. Francesc Femenies 44, tel: 971 353 798, www.bikemenorca.com). Mopeds and scooters are also available in most resorts, but you need a licence. A helmet is compulsory when riding a motorcycle. Ask the bike shop for a helmet and for a pump and puncture kit, in case you get stuck with a flat tyre.

BUDGETING FOR YOUR TRIP

All prices below are approximate and given only as a guide.

Accommodation. Rates for a double room (two sharing) in high season can range from as low as €50 per night in a *hostal* to as much as €300 at a top-of-the-range hotel. A comfortable 3-star hotel costs approximately €80–125. Rates drop considerably out of season.

Attractions. Most museums and megalithic sites charge an entry fee of around €3–4. Water parks are around €10 for under-11s, €15 for over-11s, but a family could easily spend a whole day in them.

Getting there. Air fares vary enormously. Flights from the UK with a budget airline can vary from around £95 return off-season to £220 or more in high season. From the US, flights cost approximately $900 return to Palma, from where you get a connecting flight.

Ferries. Inter-island ferries between Menorca (Ciutadella) and Mallorca (Port d'Alcúdia) cost about €85 return for foot passengers, and about €225 for a car and two passengers.

Meals. A *menú del día*, a fixed-price meal, is an excellent bargain, usually costing no more than €15 for a reasonably good three-course meal with one drink included. The average price of a three-course meal, à la carte, including house wine, will be about €30–45 per person. You can pay considerably less, but at the top restaurants you will pay a lot more *(see pages 107–13)*.

C

CAMPING *(Camping)*

Pitching a tent on beaches and parkland is illegal and a number of people are prosecuted every year for illegal camping. You may be able to camp on private land if you ask permission first.

Menorca has two official camp sites: S'Atalaia (Carretera Ferreries–Cala Galdana, tel: 971 374 232; www.campingsatalaia.com; Apr–Oct), set in pine woods 4km (2½ miles) from Ferreries and 3km (2 miles) from the beach at Cala Galdana. Son Bou (Carretera Sant Jaume–Alaior, tel: 971 372 605/971 372 727; www.camping sonbou.com; Apr–Sept), is 2.5km (1½ miles) from the beach. Facilities at both sites include a pool, showers, restaurant/bar and supermarket; advance booking is advisable.

CAR HIRE *(Coches de aquiler)*

The bus service is good, but if you want to travel around a good deal, renting a car is advisable. Major international companies – Avis, Hertz, Europcar – and Spanish national companies have offices at the airport and in Maó as well as in the major resorts. Rates are seasonal, and much lower out of season, and at any time if organised in advance, especially over the internet. You may pay around €60 a day for an economy model, but it can be a lot more; you get a much better deal if you book for a week. Third-party insurance is included by law, but comprehensive insurance – *todo riesgo* – may be extra. Insurance may not cover you for off-road driving, even in a four-wheel-drive vehicle. Most types of car are available, but the vast majority are small, economy models. Hirers must be at least 21 and have held a licence for six months. You need only your national driving licence.

I'd like to rent a car for one day/week. Please include full insurance.	**Quisiera alquilar un coche por un día/una semana. Haga el favor de incluir el seguro a todo riesgo.**

CLIMATE (Clima)

The sea is pleasantly warm for swimming from June to October. Temperatures in July and August can be scorching, and humidity may be high. Menorca enjoys a mild winter, although it can be swept by cold winds, especially in the north, where the Tramuntana can be fierce. Although many hotels still close in winter, the tourist season is getting longer: spring and autumn are mild and pleasant and popular with walkers and birdwatchers.

The chart below shows the average monthly temperatures; these do not vary greatly, except in the mountainous areas.

	J	F	M	A	M	J	J	A	S	O	N	D
°C	10	11	12	14	17	22	24	24	22	18	14	12
°F	50	51	54	58	63	71	76	76	72	65	57	53

CLOTHING (Ropa)

In summer you only need lightweight cotton clothes, although in June and September a jacket or sweater are useful for the evening. Take a sunhat and something with sleeves to cover your shoulders against the midday sun. During the rest of the year a jacket and umbrella will come in handy. Although the prevailing attitude is towards casual dress, some restaurants, bars and clubs object to men wearing shorts and T-shirts, and women being too skimpily dressed. Don't offend local sensibilities by wearing swimwear or very skimpy clothing in city streets, museums or churches. Walking shoes or trainers are advisable, of course, if you are planning long treks, as is a small backpack to carry lightweight anoraks and refreshments.

CRIME AND SAFETY (See also EMERGENCIES)

Spain's crime rate has caught up with that of other European countries, and the Balearics have not been immune, although they remain one of the safest places in Europe. Be on your guard against purse-snatchers and pickpockets around major tourist sites, and in markets and at fiestas. The rules are those you should follow anywhere. Don't leave valuables unattended, don't take them to the beach or leave them visible in a car. Make use of hotel safe-boxes where possible. Don't carry large sums of money or wear expensive jewellery, and keep hold of your camera. Be especially careful when getting money from automatic cash machines.

In Maó, report thefts and break-ins to the Policía Nacional, elsewhere to the Guardia Civil.

| I want to report a theft. | **Quiero denunciar un robo.** |

D

DRIVING (En coche)

Menorca's highway between Maó and Ciutadella, the Me-1, is very good, but can get crowded in summer. Some other roads are narrow and poorly surfaced, but great improvements have been made in recent years. Road signs are not always as clear as they might be. Be aware that there is no road running all the way round the coast.

Rules and Regulations. The rules are the same as throughout Spain: drive on the right, overtake on the left, yield to vehicles coming from the right (unless your road is marked as having priority). Seat belts are compulsory. Children under 10 must travel in the rear. You should always carry your driving licence with you, and it is a good idea to have a photocopy of your passport. Speed limits are 90km/h (56mph) on main roads, 50km/h (32mph) on minor roads, and 40km/h (25mph), unless otherwise marked, in populated areas.

Traffic police. Roads are patrolled by the Guardia Civil de Tráfico on motorbikes. They are generally courteous and helpful, but are tough on lawbreakers. Fines are payable on the spot. Don't drink and drive. The permitted blood-alcohol level is low and penalties are stiff.

Fuel. There are 11 service stations on Menorca, several grouped around the two main cities. Lead-free petrol *(gasolina)* comes in grades 90 and 98. Diesel fuel is widely available. Fuel is slightly cheaper than in the UK but will seem expensive to US visitors.

Parking. Finding a place to park can be difficult in Maó and Ciutadella, but is not a problem elsewhere. Maó, Ciutadella and Alaior have 'blue zone' metered areas, denoted by a blue 'P' and blue lines on the road. There are also some public car parks.

Mechanical problems. Garages are efficient, but repairs may take time in busy tourist areas. For emergencies, call Real Club Automóvil (tel: 971 750 110 or tel: 062).

Road signs. Most signs are the standard pictographs found throughout Europe, but the words below may be useful.

Aparcamiento	**Parking**
Desviación	**Detour**
Obras	**Road works**
Peatones	**Pedestrians**
Peligro	**Danger**
Senso único	**One way**

> **¿Se puede aparcar aquí?** Can I park here?
> **Llénelo, por favor.** Fill the tank please.
> **Ha habido un accidente.** There has been an accident.

E

ELECTRICITY (Corriente eléctrica)

The 220-v system is standard. Sockets take round, two-pin plugs, so you will need an adapter, found in UK chemists, supermarkets and at airports. US visitors will need a transformer.

EMBASSIES AND CONSULATES (Embajadas y consulados)

Canada: For minor matters contact the UK honorary consulate in Maó. In other cases, contact: Consulate General, Edificio Goya, Calle Núñez de Balboa 35, 28001 Madrid, tel: 914 233 250.

Ireland: (Honorary Consul) Carrer Sant Miquel 68, 8ª, Palma, tel: 971 719 244 or 971 722 504, or contact the UK consulate in Maó.

UK: (Honorary Consul) Camí Biniatap 30, Es Castell, Maó, tel: 971 363 373.

US: Edificio Reina Constanza, Passeig Marítim (Porto Pi), 8, 9-D, Palma, tel: 971 403 707/ 971 403 905.

> Where is the British/American **¿Dónde está el consulado**
> consulate? **británico/americano?**

EMERGENCIES (See also EMBASSIES, HEALTH and POLICE)

General emergency number (police, fire, ambulance): 112
National Police: 091
Municipal Police: 092
Guardia Civil: 062
Ambulance: 061 and Fire: 080

Police!	Policía!
Help!	Socorro!
Fire!	Fuego!
Stop!	Deténgase!

G

GAY AND LESBIAN TRAVELLERS (Viajeros gay)

The Balearics are among the most hospitable places in Spain for gay travellers. Contact Ben Amics, Carrer Arraval, 71, Maó, tel: 971 715 670, www.benamics.com.

GETTING THERE

Air Travel (*see page 116*). Menorca's airport is linked by regular scheduled flights with London, Berlin, Frankfurt and other European cities but some of them, including Iberia, British Airways, bmi and Air Europa go via Barcelona, Madrid or Palma. Monarch flies direct from Gatwick, Luton, Birmingham and Manchester. From Dublin, flights go via Barcelona or Palma. Flights from the US and Canada go via Barcelona or Madrid and then on to Palma. Flight time from the UK (direct) is about 2½ hours; from New York approximately 10 hours, from Los Angeles 12 hours. From Australia and New Zealand, you go via London to Madrid or Barcelona, then get a connecting flight.

For scheduled flights from the UK, contact Iberia (tel: 0870-609 0500 or 1-800-772 4642, www.iberia.com), British Airways (tel: 0844-493 0787, www.britishairways.com) or Monarch Airlines (tel: 08719-405 040, www.monarch.co.uk). From Eire, contact Aer Lingus (tel: 0818 365 044, www.aerlingus.com). The website of Opodo (www.opodo.com) finds the best flights operated by a number of major airlines.

In the US contact Iberia (tel: 1-800 772 4642, www.iberia. com),

British Airways (tel: 1-800 247 9297, www.britishair ways.com) or
Continental Airlines (tel: 1-800 231 0856, www.continental.com).
In Canada, contact British Airways (tel: 1-800 247 9297) or Iberia
(tel: 1-800 423 7421).Website addresses as above.

Easyjet (www.easyjet.com) flies from UK airports to Palma from
where you get a connecting flight, and in summer flies from Gatwick
direct to Maó three times a week. Flights from Palma to Maó take
45 minutes and cost around €95 return.

By Sea. Passenger hydrofoil services (the Balearjet) between Mallorca and Menorca run between Cala Ratjada and Ciutadella (Cape
Balear, tel: 902 100 444, www.interilles.es). The journey takes about
1 hour. Car ferries run twice a day (except Saturday) between Port
d'Alcúdia and Ciutadella and take around 2 hours 45 minutes (Is-
comar Ferries, tel: 902 119 128/971 437 500, www.iscomar.com).

In summer there are daily direct links from Barcelona to Maó via
Acciona-Trasmediterránea, journey time about 9 hours; off-season
the service runs three times a week. There's also a weekly summer
service between Valencia and Maó, journey time about 14 hours
(tel: 902 454 645, www.trasmediterranea.es for both). There is also
a Baleària service between Barcelona and Maó (9 hours); and in
summer between Barcelona and Ciutadella on a fast ferry, *Ramon
Llull* (about 4 hours), tel: 902 160 180, www.balearia.net.

H

HEALTH AND MEDICAL CARE *(Salud; atención médica)*

Standards of hygiene on Menorca are generally high; the most
common problems visitors encounter are due to an excess of sun
or alcohol. Bottled water is always safest, and is available everywhere. *Agua con gas* is carbonated water; *agua sin gas* is still.

There are doctors' surgeries in all towns: look for the Centro de
Salud or Consultorio Local. For less serious matters, first-aid

personnel (called *practicantes*) make daily rounds of the larger resort hotels. Many resorts have medical centres *(centros medicos)*, privately run institutions that must be paid on the spot, in cash or by credit card (roughly €50/£44 per consultation). The Salus Medical Centres (freephone: 900 711 711) have clinics all over the island, and staff speak both English and German.

There is a good modern general hospital in Maó: Hospital Mateu Orfila, Ronda Malbúger 13, tel: 971 487 000, emergencies tel: 971 487 030, and the private Policlínica Virgen de Gràcia (Carrer Vives Llull 6, tel: 971 351 115). In Ciutadella there's the public Centro de Salud Canal Salat (Carrer Sant Antoni M. Claret, tel: 971 480 112), and the private Clínica Menorca (Canonge Moll, tel: 971 480 505). All open 24 hours for emergencies.

It is always advisable to take out insurance to cover illness or accident. EU residents are entitled to reciprocal health arrangements on production of the European health insurance card (EHIC), available free in your home country, but it does not cover all eventualities.

Pharmacies *(farmácias)* are open during shopping hours, but there is at least one – the *farmácia de guardia* – open all night in Maó and Ciutadella. In smaller towns, it may be difficult to find an after-hours pharmacy. A list showing the pharmacy on rota duty is posted in chemists' windows. Spanish pharmacists are highly trained and generally speak some English.

Emergency medical assistance can be obtained by contacting the

Where's the nearest (all-night) chemist?	¿Dónde está la farmácia (de guardia) más cercana?
I need a doctor/ dentist	Necesito un médico/ dentista.
sunburn/ sunstroke	quemadura del sol/ una insolación
an upset stomach	molestias de estómago

Red Cross (Cruz Roja), tel: 112 or 971 361 180 (Maó), tel: 971 381 993 (Ciutadella).

HOLIDAYS *(Fiestas)*

The following are official public holidays. There are a number of other regional holidays, usually saints' days, dotted throughout the year; tourist offices will tell you when the main ones are.

1 January	*Año Nuevo*	New Year's Day
6 January	*Epifanía*	Epiphany
20 January	*San Sebastián*	St Sebastian's Day
1 May	*Día del Trabajo*	Labour Day
25 July	*Santiago Apóstol*	St James's Day
15 August	*Asunción*	Assumption
12 October	*Día de la Hispanidad*	National Day
1 November	*Todos los Santos*	All Saints' Day
6 December	*Día de la Española*	Constitution Day
8 December	*Inmaculada Concepción*	Immaculate Conception
25 December	*Navidad*	Christmas Day

Movable dates:

Late March/April	*Jueves Santo*	Maundy Thursday
Late March/April	*Viernes Santo*	Good Friday
Late March/April	*Lunes de Pascua*	Easter Monday
Mid-June	*Corpus Christi*	Corpus Christi

L

LANGUAGE *(Idioma; lenguaje)*

While Castilian Spanish is the national language, a local form of Catalan – Menorquí – is now the official language of the island and is more widely spoken; however, almost all islanders speak both. Most street signs appear only in Catalan, although the names of some establishments often seem to be a mixture of the two languages and some older people still use the Spanish names. If you know some Spanish, you'll be fine; the effort to speak Catalan is appreciated, but it is not necessary. English and German are widely understood in resort areas, and making oneself undersood is rarely a problem.

The *Berlitz Spanish–English/English–Spanish Pocket Dictionary* covers most situations you're likely to encounter.

Do you speak English?	**¿Habla usted inglés?**
I don't speak Spanish.	**No hablo español.**

M

MAPS *(Mapa = country/regional map; plano = town map)*

The map of the island produced by the tourist board and available at all tourist information offices should be sufficient, even for those travelling by car. Just make sure you are clear which are rough tracks and which asphalted roads, as the distinction on maps is not always as obvious as it might be. The tourist office in Maó provides excellent little maps of the two cities. A good place for more specific maps and books on the island is Fundació (Carrer Hannover, Costa de Sa Plaça 14, Maó).

Do you have a map of the city/island?	**¿Tiene un plano de la a ciudad/isla?**

MEDIA *(Periódico = newspaper; revista = magazine)*

In main tourist areas most English and German newspapers are sold on the day of publication during the summer months. The Paris-based *International Herald Tribune* and the European edition of the *Wall Street Journal* are also available, as are the principal European and American magazines. The Menorca English-language magazine

Roqueta has a 'What's On' section. For Spanish speakers, the *Diario de Menorca*, the Menorca edition of *Última Hora* and all Spanish national papers and magazines are available.

Most hotels and bars have television, usually tuned to sports, and broadcasting in Castilian, Catalan and Menorquí. Satellite dishes are sprouting and most tourist hotels offer multiple channels (German, French, Sky, BBC, CNN, etc). Reception of Britain's BBC World Service radio is usually good. A good set will (sometimes) receive BBC long-wave and even medium-wave domestic programmes.

MONEY *(Dinero)*

Currency. Spain's monetary unit is the euro (€), which is divided into 100 cents. Bank notes are available in denominations of 5, 10, 20, 50, 100, 200 and 500 euros, and there are coins for 1 and 2 euros and for 1, 2, 5, 10, 20 and 50 cents.

Currency exchange. Banks offer the best rates and do not charge commission. A large number of travel agencies exchange foreign currency, and *casas de cambio (*exchange offices) stay open outside banking hours. Be wary of those advertising 'no commission' – their rates are considerably lower than those offered elsewhere, so you are in effect paying a hefty commission. Both banks and exchange offices pay slightly less for cash than for traveller's cheques. Always take your passport as proof of identity.

Credit cards. Major international credit cards are widely recognised, although smaller businesses tend to prefer cash. Visa/Eurocard/MasterCard are the most widely accepted. Credit and debit cards are also useful for obtaining cash from ATMs – cash machines – which are found in all towns and resorts. They offer the most convenient way of obtaining cash and will usually give you the best exchange rate.

Travellers' Cheques. The majority of hotels and travel agencies cash travellers cheques, and so do banks, where you're likely to get a better rate (you need your passport). Always keep a note of your unused cheque numbers somewhere safe and separate from the cheques, in case of theft or loss.

Where's the nearest bank/ currency exchange office?	¿Dónde está el banco más cercano/la oficina de cambio más cercana?
I want to change some dollars/pounds.	Quiero cambiar dólares/ libres esterlina.
Do you accept travellers' cheques?	¿Acepta usted cheques de viajero?
Can I pay with this credit card?	¿Puedo pagar con esta tarjeta de crédito?

O

OPENING TIMES

Shops and offices: 9.30am–1.30pm and 5–8pm. Large supermarkets and department stores usually open all day, and some until 10pm.
Museums and other attractions: the hours of the major museums are given in the relevant section of this guide. Many close on Monday, and also for a longish midday break.
Post offices: Monday to Friday 9am–1.30pm.
Banks: Monday–Friday 9am–1.30pm, and also Saturday 9am–1pm in winter.
Restaurants: lunch from 1–3.30pm, dinner 8–11pm *(for more detail see pages 103–4)*.

P

POLICE *(Policía)*

Spanish municipal and national police are efficient, strict and courteous, and generally very responsive to issues involving tourists.

The general emergency number for all services is 112. Dial 092 for municipal police and 091 for national police. The municipal police station in Maó can be contacted on tel: 971 363 712, in Ciutadella, tel: 971 381 095.

POST OFFICES *(Correos)*

Identified by yellow-and-white signs with a crown and the words *Correos y Telégrafos*, post offices are for mail and telegrams; you can't telephone from them. Check www.correos.es for information. The postal system is pretty reliable and efficient. Opening hours are usually Monday to Friday 9am–1.30pm. The main post office in Maó is on Carrer Bon Aire, tel: 971 363 892; in Ciutadella, it is in Plaça des Born, tel: 971 380 081. Stamps *(sellos)* are also sold by tobacconist's *(estancos/tabacos)* and by most shops selling postcards, although they do appreciate it if you buy your postcards there, too.

Where is the (nearest) post office?	**¿Dónde está la oficina de correos (más cercana)?**
A stamp for this letter/ postcard, please.	**Por favor, un sello para esta carta/tarjeta.**

PUBLIC TRANSPORT *(Transporte público)*

Bus *(autobus)*. Regular bus services run from Maó and Ciutadella to most towns and resorts. The vehicles are clean and easy to use, fares are reasonable, and drivers are generally friendly and helpful. Destinations are marked on the front of the buses. In Maó, most buses start from the terminal in Carrer Vassallo behind Plaça de s'Esplanada (ask for the *estación de autobuses*). Contact Transportes Menorca (TMSA), tel: 971 360 475, www.tmsa.es. In Ciutadella, most services commence at the terminal in Plaça des Pins (beside Plaça des Born). It is not so easy to travel between smaller towns by bus – you usually have to return to one of the two main terminals, which can make relatively short distances take quite a long time. The airport bus is run by a different company, Torres (tel: 902 075 066, www.e-torres.net).

Taxi. Taxi prices in Menorca compare favourably with those in many countries. Check the fare before you get in; rates are fixed and are displayed in several languages on the windows. Hotel reception staff will always book taxis for you, but a few useful phone numbers are: Maó: Radio Taxi (tel: 971 367 111), taxi stand in Plaça d'España (tel: 971 362 891), in Plaça de s'Esplanada (tel: 971 361 283). In Ciutadella, try: Radio Taxi (tel: 971 382 896), taxi stand in Avinguda Constitució (tel: 971 381 197), in Plaça d'es Born (tel: 971 384 435) and in Sant Lluis (tel: 971 150 641).

Train. There is no train service on the island.

T

TELEPHONES *(Teléfonos)*

Spain's country code is 34. The local area code, 971, must be dialled before all phone numbers, even for local calls.

The telephone office is independent of the post office and is identified by a blue-and-white sign. You can make direct-dial local and international calls from public telephone booths *(cabinas)* in the street. Some accept both coins and cards but card-only phones are more prevalent; international phone cards and credit cards can also be used. You can buy a a phone card *(tarjeta telefónica)* in various denominations at any *estanco* (tobacconist's shop). Instructions for use are given in several languages in the booths. In Maó, Ciutadella and some of the bigger resorts you can also use public telephone offices called *locutorios*. This is quieter than making a call on the street, and more convenient, as you pay afterwards. To make an international call, dial 00, then the country code plus the phone number, omitting any initial zero. Calls are cheapest after 10pm on weekdays, after 2pm on Saturday, and all day Sunday.

TIME ZONES *(Huso horario)*

The Balearics keep the same time as mainland Spain, which is one hour ahead of GMT. Spanish time is hence generally one hour ahead of London, the same as Paris and six hours ahead of New York.

TIPPING *(Propinas)*

A service charge is sometimes included on restaurant bills (look for the words *servicio incluido*). If not, it is usual to tip waiters 10 percent and taxi drivers a similar amount; it's normal to leave a few coins, rounding up the bill, at a bar counter. Porters, hairdressers and chambermaids should be given €1–2.

TOILETS *(Servicios)*

There are many expressions for toilets in Spanish: *servicios, aseos* or *lavabos* are the most commonly used. Toilet doors usually have a 'C' for Caballeros (Gentlemen), or an 'S' for Señoras (Ladies). Public toilets exist in some large towns but they are rare; most bars will allow you to use their facilities without asking if you are a customer. Those that object usually keep the key behind the bar so you have to ask for it.

TOURIST INFORMATION OFFICES
(Oficinas de información turística)

Before leaving, you can get information from the Spanish Tourist Office in your home country:

Canada: 2 Bloor Street West, Suite 3402, Toronto, Ontario M4W 3E2, tel: 1416-961 3131, www.tourspaintoronto.on.ca.
UK: 79 New Cavendish Street, London W1W 6SB, visits by appointment only, tel: 020 7486 8077, information line tel: 0870-850 6599, www.spain.info.
US: Water Tower Place, Suite 915 East, 845 North Michigan Avenue, Chicago, IL 60611, tel: 312-642 1992.

8383 Wilshire Boulevard, Suite 960, Beverly Hills, CA 90211, tel: 213-658 7188.
666 5th Avenue, 35th floor, New York, NY 10103, tel: 212-265 8822. US website for all three offices: www.okspain.org.

Tourist Offices in Menorca
There is a new, multilingual, island-wide tourist information line, tel: 902 929 015. The main tourist offices are:
Maó: Estación Central de Autobuses, Avinguda Anselm Clavé, Maó, tel: 971 363 790, email: infomenorcamao@menorca.es; Moll de Levant 2, tel: 971 355 952, email: infomenorcaport@menorca.es. Aeroport de Maó, Arrivals Hall, tel: 902 929 015, email: info menorcaeroport@menorca.es.
Ciutadella: Plaça de la Catedral 5, tel: 971 382 693, email: info menorcaciutadella@cime.es; Plaça d'es Born, tel: 971 484 155, email: infomenorcaciutadella@menorca.es.

There are offices in many other resorts and towns, although they are usually only open in summer. Staff are usually helpful and speak some English or German. They may have lists of hotels but do not as a rule assist with finding accommodation.

TRAVELLERS WITH DISABILITIES *(Los discapacitados)*

The Balearic Islands, like mainland Spain, are becoming increasingly geared up to receiving visitors with disabilities these days. Maó airport and most large modern hotels have wheelchair access and facilities for travellers with disabilities, although visiting some churches and museums/galleries and negotiating narrow streets may present more of a problem. For general information, consult the online *Able Magazine*, 15–39 Durham Street, Kinning Park, Glasgow GW1 1BS, tel: 0141 419 0044, www.ablemagazine.co.uk.

Tourism for All (tel: 0845 124 9971, www.tourismforall.org.uk) also provides information for travellers with disabilities.

V

VISAS AND ENTRY REQUIREMENTS (see also Embassies and Consulates)

Citizens of the UK, the US, Canada, Australia and New Zealand need only a valid passport to enter Spain and the Balearics, for a stay of up to 90 days. Citizens of South Africa need a visa. Full information on passport and visa regulations is available from the Spanish Embassy in your own country.

As Spain is part of the European Union (EU), free exchange of non-duty-free items for personal use is permitted between Spain and other EU countries. However, duty-free items are still subject to restrictions. There are no limits on the amount of money that you may import, but you should declare sums over the equivalent of €30,000.

W

WEBSITES AND INTERNET ACCESS

www.illesbalears.es (useful site for general information, museums, outdoor activities and much more)
http://menorca.costasur.com (general information including accommodation, transport and useful phone numbers)
www.menorcaweb.com (art, culture, accommodation, transport, eating, shopping, entertainment)
www.emenorca.org (basic information, but good on environmental and conservation matters)
www.visitmenorca.com (Menorca Hotel Association site. Gives general information as well as hotel reservations)
There are internet cafés in Maó, Ciutadella and the main resorts. They come and go but the current ones are usually prominently advertised. Note that the availability of Wi-fi in many hotels means there are fewer internet cafés than there used to be.

Recommended Hotels

There is a wide range of accommodation available on Menorca, from luxury hotels to small, family-run hostels, as well as the huge, impersonal, but efficient modern hotels in the resorts, where much of the accommodation is block-booked by tour companies. Officially, establishments are classified as *pensiónes*, *hostales* or *hoteles*, but the lines between them are often blurred. Prices drop considerably out of season, but many hotels close between November and Easter, so the cheaper periods are usually from mid-April to mid-June and mid-September to the end of October. Finding winter accommodation isn't always easy and places that stay open all year will be indicated in the listings below. For details on rural *(agroturismo)* holidays, see page 115.

A growing number of establishments include a buffet breakfast in the quoted price; some rates also include IVA, the 8 percent value-added tax on hotel rooms, but it is not standard, so it is wise to check. Web addresses are given only when they are specific to the hotel, rather than reservation agencies. In the listings, the following ranges are used to indicate prices for a double room per night in high season and are given as a guide only:

€€€€	over 250 euros
€€€	125–250 euros
€€	75–125 euros
€	below 75 euros

MAÓ AND ES CASTELL

Almirante €€ *Carretera Maó–Es Castell, tel: 971 362 700, www. hoteldelalmirante.com.* A friendly, somewhat old-fashioned hotel in a Georgian mansion built for Nelson's right-hand man, Lord Collingwood. There are 10 antique-furnished bedrooms and a lounge in the main hotel, and 30 other rooms built hacienda-style around a garden and pool. There's a tennis court, billiard room and massage facilities. Situated half way between Maó and Es Castell. Special terms for regular guests, of whom there are many.

Barceló Hamilton €€ *Passeig Santa Agueda 6, Es Castell, tel: 971 362 050, www.barcelohamilton.com.* This big modern hotel by the harbour has 166 rooms, most with sea views; there is also a pool and a buffet restaurant. It is largely booked by tour groups but has some rooms available for individual travellers. All-inclusive and full-board terms are available. Open all year.

Capri €€ *Carrer Sant Esteve 8, tel: 902 356 935, www.artiemhotels. com/en-menorca/hotel-capri/the-hotel.html.* Modern, efficient and comfortable, if somewhat characterless, the Capri, part of the Artiem chain, is close to the Plaça de s'Esplanada. The glass-enclosed pool and jacuzzi have views over the city. This hotel caters to pre-booked groups. Open all year.

Hostal-Residencia Jume € *Carrer Concepció 6, tel: 971 363 266, email: reservas@hostaljume.com.* In a large, modern block near Plaça de Miranda, the Jume offers basic rooms, with bathrooms and breakfast included for a modest price. There's an extra 2.5 percent charge if you pay by credit card. Closed Christmas period only.

La Isla € *Carrer Santa Catalina 4, tel: 971 366 492.* A basic but friendly *hostal* in a narrow street to the east of the centre. All 22 rooms are en suite and have televisions. There's also a bar and restaurant downstairs. Closed mid-Dec–mid-Jan.

Port Mahón €€€ *Avinguda Fort de l'Eau 13, tel: 971 362 600, www.sethotels.com/en/hotel-port-mahon-menorca.php.* A splendid rusty-red colonial-style mansion overlooking the harbour, about 15 minutes' walk from the centre. Comfortable, air-conditioned rooms, most with balconies; excellent service, pool, terrace bar, restaurant and lovely gardens. Open all year.

Posada Orsi € *Carretera Infanta 19, tel: 971 364 751, www.posada orsi.es.* Centrally located, this small, simple and efficient *hostal* in a typical Menorcan house has rooms decorated with attractive ethnic touches and a 'chill-out room' in primary colours. One room has a roof terrace with an amazing view. Some rooms have their own bathrooms, while others are shared.

Almirante Farragut € *Cala en Forcat, tel: 971 388 000.* Right by the sea with great views over the bay, the hotel offers comfortable air-conditioned rooms, an outdoor pool and a tennis court. Represents good value for the moderate price.

Ciutadella €–€€ *Carrer Sant Eloi 10, tel: 971 383 462.* Located close to the Plaça de Ses Palmeras this modest but comfortable little place is good value and has its own restaurant. Open all year.

Esmeralda €€ *Passeig Sant Nicolau 175, tel: 971 380 250.* The concrete bulk, sinuous lines and blue balconies make this well-equipped hotel opposite Castell de Sant Nicolau unmissable. Many rooms have balconies with harbour views. There is also a large pool and tennis courts, and it offers a programme of sporting activities. Mostly booked by tour groups. Closed Nov–Dec.

Hesperia Patricia €€ *Passeig Sant Nicolau 90–2, tel: 971 385 511, www.hesperia.es.* A modern, comfortable and well-appointed hotel in a quiet street close to the port and only a few minutes' walk from Plaça d'es Born. Business centre and conference facilities. The Sa Cúpula restaurant (breakfast and lunch only) is recommended. Small pool.

Hotel Rural Biniatram €€€ *Carretera Cala Morell, tel: 971 383 113, www.biniatram.com.* This is a traditional Menorcan *finca*, whose origins go back 500 years. In peaceful countryside just outside Cala Morell, only 7km (4 miles) from Ciutadella, the hotel is set in beautiful gardens. Amenities include a large pool and tennis court. Breakfast not included in the price. Also rents apartments.

Hotel Rural Sant Ignasi €€€–€€€€ *Carretera Cala Morell, tel: 971 385 575, www.santignasi.com.* This 18th-century manor house, set in farmland 4km (2½ miles) north of Ciutadella, manages to be both rustic and elegant. Each room is different – all are furnished with antiques, while some have huge terraces. There's an excellent restaurant and an inviting bar and pool. Closed mid-Dec–mid-Jan.

Madrid € *Carrer Madrid 60, tel: 971 380 328*. In a quiet street 10 minutes' walk from Plaça d'es Born, this little hostal is basic and friendly. All 22 rooms are en suite and have balconies, some with harbour views. There's a bar, cafeteria and a small pool – although the pool is right by the road.

Morvedra Nou €€€ *Camí de Sant Joan de Missa Km 7, tel: 971 359 521/971 359 512, www.morvedranou.es*. A 17th-century house offers comfortable accommodation in a rural atmosphere. Set in peaceful countryside with splendid views, only 7km (4 miles) from Ciutadella and about the same from the beaches of Cala Turqueta and Cala Macarella. Pool and gardens. Horse riding excursions can be organised.

Port de Ciutadella €€€ *Passeig Marítim 36, tel: 971 482 520, www.sethotels.com/es/hotel-port-ciutadella-menorca.php*. A luxurious hotel close to Platja Gran, with 94 rooms and 18 suites furnished in minimalist style, all with broadband access. Pool, spa, gym and conference facilities.

Sa Prensa € *Carrer Madrid s/n, tel: 971 382 698*. Sa Prensa is an unpretentious and functional *hostal* on the next block from the Madrid *(see above)*. The eight double rooms are all en suite and some have balconies with sea views. There is a café and bar on the ground floor.

THE NORTHEAST

FORNELLS

Hostal Fornells €€ *Carrer Major 17, tel: 971 376 676, www.hostalfornells.com*. Attractive and friendly hotel that calls itself an 'eco resort'. The 23 rooms are comfortably furnished, as are the public areas, and 12 rooms have sea views. Excellent breakfasts included; exercise and nutrition programmes can be arranged. The pool is surrounded by a pleasant sunbathing area.

Hostal La Palma €€ *Plaça S'Algaret 3, tel: 971 376 634, www.hostallapalma.com*. Right by the harbour, this friendly place has simply furnished rooms, some overlooking the sea, others with views of garden and small pool. There's a busy local bar on the ground floor. Apartments are available for rent in winter, when the hotel is otherwise closed.

Hostal Residencia Port Fornells €€ *Urbanización Ses Salines, tel: 971 376 373, www.hostalportfornells.com.* The location on the lagoon in the Ses Salines development, just south of town, makes this easy-going place popular with windsurfers.

Hostal S'Algaret €€ *Plaça S'Algaret 7, tel: 971 376 552/971 376 499, www.hostal-salgaret.com.* This hotel offers functional, plain and pleasant rooms, as well as a small pool. There are harbour views from the first-floor restaurant's floor-to-ceiling windows and rooms have small terraces with garden/pool views.

THE SOUTH

BINIBECA VELL

Complejo Binivell Parc €€ *Urbanización Binibeca Vell, tel: 971 150 608, reservations tel: 902 112 010.* There are apartments and studios to rent in this twee but pretty architect-designed 'fishermen's village'. Rates include services and cleaning.

CALA BLANCA

Cala Blanca €€ *Urbanización Cala Blanca, tel: 971 380 450.* This hotel is set on a quiet pine-lined road at the edge of the development, close to the sea and open countryside. It offers comfortable rooms, a large pool, outdoor activities, indoor entertainment and 24-hour medical services, mostly on an all-inclusive basis. Car, bike and moped hire can also be arranged.

Globales Hotel Mediterrani €€ *Urbanización Cala Blanca, tel: 902 106 118.* The Mediterrani is high-rise, modern and not very beautiful, however, the 180 air-conditioned rooms are comfortable and have large balconies, the service is good, and the hotel is very close to the beach. It is mostly booked by tour groups but there are usually some rooms available for individual travellers.

CALA EN BOSC

La Quinta €€€€ *Carrer des Port s/n, tel: 902 575 268, http://salgar hotels.com/es/vacaciones-de-lujo-menorca-hotel-la-quita.html.* A five-star spa hotel in a colonial-style building, furnished with traditional materials, close to the beaches of Son Xoriguer and Cala en Bosc. As well as a large outdoor pool, it has a heated indoor pool and Turkish bath and offers water massage treatments. A place to go if you want to be pampered.

CALA N'PORTER

IBB Aquarium €€ *Passeig de la Platja, tel: 971 377 077/971 356 869.* This is a medium-sized, featureless modern hotel with a large pool, but it is right by the beach and the mouth of the gorge, so there is no trekking up and down the hill. Offers only half-board accommodation.

CALA SANTA GALDANA

Cala Galdana and Villas d'Aljandar €€€ *Passeig Marítim, tel: 971 154 500, www.hotelcalagaldana.com.* A large, efficient, international-style hotel on the road paralleling the river. Caters largely to tour groups but does have rooms for individual guests. Live entertainment, gym, children's playground and four restaurants. Minimum three-night stay in high season. Also has an attractive apartment-bungalow complex.

Rtm Audax Spa & Wellness Centre €€€ *Cala Santa Galdana, tel: 902 356 935, www.artiemhotels.com.* A large, modern hotel, the Audax has 244 air-conditioned rooms with balconies and views of either the sea, the pool or pine woods. Facilities include a gym, sauna, jacuzzi and hair salon. The hotel can organise all kinds of outdoor activities, from canoeing to hiking and archery.

Sol Elite Gavilanes €€€ *Cala Santa Galdana, tel: 971 154 545, www.solmelia.com/hotels/spain/menorca/sol-gavilanes/home.htm.* A massive pile dominating the bay. Its own views are splendid, even if they rather spoil other people's. It is a comfortable place to stay and the service is efficient; there are three restaurants, two pools and sports facilities.

SANT LLUÍS

Biniarroca Hotel Rural €€€ *Camí Vell, Carretera Sant Lluís–Es Castell, tel: 971 150 059, www.biniarroca.com.* This 15th-century farmhouse has been lovingly converted into an elegant country hotel. The rooms have period furniture, and original oil paintings on the walls. There are peaceful gardens, an attractive pool and an award-winning restaurant. Offers special deals in April and May.

Binissafullet Vell €€€ *Carretera Binissafullet 64, tel: 971 156 633, www.binissafullet.com.* An attractive rural *agroturismo* property set in leafy gardens with a small pool. Eight well-furnished rooms with beamed ceilings. Open all year.

Hotel S'Algar €€€ *Urbanización S'Algar, tel: 902 575 268.* An attractive spot with whitewashed arched buildings, a large pool, a spa, sea views and lovely gardens. Contains 106 rooms with terraces. Free Wi-fi in public areas.

SANT TOMÀS

Santo Tomàs €€€ *Urbanización Sant Tomás, tel: 971 370 025.* Vey close to the beach, this modern, streamlined hotel has 85 air-conditioned rooms, each with a small balcony or terrace. There is an indoor heated pool for cooler days.

SON BOU

Hotel Valentín Son Bou €€ *Urbanización Torre Solí Nou, tel: 971 372 602.* The low-rise four-star Hotel Valentín is set on a slight hill above the resort of Son Bou, surrounded by pine trees. It's a family-friendly place with helpful staff. Apartments are also available for guests who prefer self-catering. Note that there is a six-night minimum stay in high season.

Sol Pinguinos Milanos *Platja Son Bou, tel: 971 371 200, email: sol.milanos.pinguinos@solmelia.com.* A monolithic monster right by the beach. The rooms of these two adjoining hotels have balconies and there are all the modern conveniences and facilities you would expect from such an immense complex, including children's amusements.

THE CENTRE

ES MERCADAL

Hostal Jeni €€ *Carrer Mirador del Toro 81, tel: 971 375 059/971 375 124, www.hostaljeni.de.* In a big ochre-coloured building at the east end of the town is this simple but very pleasant *hostal*. There's a heated pool with a retractable roof and a good restaurant serving imaginative *cuina menorquina*. Recent renovation has equipped the hotel with facilities for people with disabilities. Two-night minimum stay in high season.

ES MIGJORN GRAN

Las Palmeras € *Carrer Major 85, tel: 971 370 023.* Las Palmeras is a simple guest house located close to the church in the main street of this attractive little town. You won't find any frills here, but it's spotlessly clean and the atmosphere is very friendly. And, if you've booked in advance, you can eat at S'Engolidor just down the road *(see below and page 113).*

S'Engolidor €–€€ *Carrer Major 3, tel: 971 370 193.* Four delight-fully old-fashioned en suite rooms in an 18th-century house, furnished with antiques and knick-knacks. There is no name out-side to tell you that this is a hotel – just look for the house number. S'Engolidor also has a splendid and well-known restaurant serving Menorcan dishes in a delightful dining room or on an outside ter-race *(see page 113).*

FERRERIES

Son Triay Nou €€ *Carretera Santa Galdana Km 3, tel: 971 155 078, www.sontriay.com.* This distinctive pink colonial-style build-ing, about 3km (2 miles) from Ferreries and 4km (3 miles) from Cala Santa Galdana, is a friendly and relaxing place to stay, and makes a good starting point for walks in the nearby Barranc d'Al-gendar. Set in extensive grounds, it has a pool and tennis court. Breakfast usually includes sausages and cheese made on the premises. There are just five attractively furnished rooms and six apartments. Apartments available all year, hotel rooms from Apr–Oct only.

INDEX

Berlitz pocket guide

Menorca

Third Edition 2012
Reprinted 2013

Written and updated by Pam Barrett
Project Manager: Catherine Dreghorn
Series Editor: Tom Stainer

Photography credits
All photography courtesy of Menorca Tourist
Board except AWL Images 99; Stephane
Benito/Fotolia 5TR; Fotolia 4BL, 62; Gladman
4–5; Anibal Trejo/Fotolia 8; Ignasi Angrill Valles
5BR

Cover picture: 4Corners Images

Every effort has been made to provide
accurate information in this publication,
but changes are inevitable. The publisher
cannot be responsible for any resulting
loss, inconvenience or injury.

Contact us

At Berlitz we strive to keep our guides as
accurate and up to date as possible, but if you
find anything that has changed, or if you have any
suggestions on ways to improve this guide, then
we would be delighted to hear from you.

Berlitz Publishing, PO Box 7910,
London SE1 1WE, England.
email: berlitz@apaguide.co.uk
www.insightguides.com/berlitz